ISBN 978-1-332-11515-0
PIBN 10286673

1 MONTH OF
FREE
READING

at
www.ForgottenBooks.com

---◆---

By purchasing this book you are eligible for one month membership to ForgottenBooks.com, giving you unlimited access to our entire collection of over 1,000,000 titles via our web site and mobile apps.

To claim your free month visit:

www.forgottenbooks.com/free286673

A COMPLETE COURSE IN MILLINERY

Twenty-four Practical Lessons Detailing the Processes for Mastering the

ART OF MILLINERY

A Text Book for Teachers of Millinery. A Guide for the Millinery Workroom. Especially Compiled to Provide Complete and Practical Lessons for the Student in Shop or School or at Home. Incorporates all the methods which experienced Milliners employ to lighten their tasks and make easy the most difficult processes

Founded on Lessons in Millinery from
THE ILLUSTRATED MILLINER, NEW YORK

Arranged by Julia Bottomley, 1914

Revised by
Emma Maxwell Burke, 1919

Published by

THE ILLUSTRATED MILLINER CO.
NEW YORK

A COMPLETE COURSE IN MILLINERY

INDEX TO LESSONS

3

MARIE ANTOINETTE WITH A ROSE

Portrait painted by Mme. Vigée Lebrun, now in the Louvre, Paris

Marie Antoinette, Louis XVI's queen, introduced the turban, ever since a favored form of headdress. This highly ornate turban was created by the court milliner. Rose Bertin. How highly the queen esteemed this headdress is evidenced by her selecting it when posing for this portrait, which she realized would perpetuate, not only her features, but her taste in dress as well. This turban is universally recognized by artists as a classic in composition, though combining a multitude of different trimmings: there are employed plumes, a metallic flower, a jewelled cabochon, ribbons, lace, gauze and velvet. Beauty of contour and faultless taste are maintained, notwithstanding.

PREPARATION FOR LESSONS

Light—Necessary Supplies—Tools

When taking up the study of millinery, one should approach it neither with fear nor an overconfidence.

A lady once said, "To see a velvet hat, its perfect binding, its artistic folds, its smooth surfaces and delicate curves, with never a stitch showing, nor a hint of its supporting structure, fills me with awe, as in the presence of a "mystery."

But be it remembered that what has been done .by one human being, in all ordinary cases, can be accomplished by another, with persistence and care.

The hat is not made at one "fell bound," but little by little the art is acquired, each step following the last in natural sequence and each step neither difficult nor unpleasant.

To approach the subject in this spirit is never to feel fear.

The overconfidence usually comes with the *natural milliner*. There is no such person! One may possess a natural aptitude for the art, but when the assumption is made that the person in question "only needs a lesson or two, for she makes all our hats at home," you can safely depend upon the fact *that the hats look it!*

A man may deem himself a natural carpenter, but he does not dare to build a house until he has learned how to lay the foundation, raise the superstructure, put in the chimney, weatherboard and roof it, and then the interior finish has to come afterward.

In making a hat, it is equally necessary that a person be skilled in making the frame, strongly bracing it, padding the edge, and then putting on the velvet, silk or braid, in a workmanlike way. The finishing comes on the outside, in the choice of trimming, which must be made in a certain manner, and arranged for artistic effect.

The "natural milliner" is especially hard to teach, because of preconceived opinions, which are usually wrong. So the first step is to *unlearn* before beginning instruction.

Taste and ability vary in individuals, and no one is so glad to discover one or both as the instructor, who will do everything in her power to develop them.

These lessons are in daily use in hundreds of classes in Domestic

Arts, in school everywhere. They have been most carefully revised for this edition. Thousands of students have qualified for the trade, hundreds have opened businesses of their own. Others have used the lessons for self-instruction. All have been equally successful.

If each of these lessons is mastered in turn, the next one will not be difficult. With an open mind and cheerful heart we will now look to the necessities for beginning.

Good Light Very Essential

Light is the first requisite. *Light,* and lots of it. Not the direct rays of the sun, but a strong light diffused through a thin curtain or frosted glass. The position is preferable if the light could fall over the left shoulder.

A table for our work is the next consideration. A plain kitchen table with a drawer fills all requirements. Cover it with a sheet or some white cotton cloth, doubled several times. Be careful that the cloth has no nap to rub off on velvet. Secure the cloth by a few tacks underneath the table edge. These can be easily removed so that the cloth can be washed.

Do not make the mistake of using oilcloth, for no oilcloth made but will gather an infinitesimal dust, which will show on white velvet or a clean duster, when it is rubbed over the oilcloth surface.

Have a comfortable chair, low enough, so the feet come squarely on the floor, without undue pressure on the edge of the seat. For one who sits long hours too much care cannot be given to the nature of the chair. The old fashioned wooden Windsor chair is preferable to any other because the seat never sags, causing pressure on the edge. If the seat is too hard, use a thin cushion.

The table should be furnished with a small piece of hard wood into which have been driven a half dozen headless wire nails for a spool rack. The wood should be sufficiently heavy and broad to hold the spools upright and not turn over. This rack will hold the four spools which will be enumerated later, and the two empty nails are for colored thread, as it may be needed.

A flat tray for pins is better than a cushion, for when the pins are being taken out of a piece of work it is very much easier to put them on a tray than to stick them in a cushion, and they are no harder to get when used.

6

A COMPLETE COURSE IN MILLINERY

The following list comprises the necessary furnishings for a beginner:

    1 spool of white millinery thread No. 24
    1 spool of black millinery thread No. 24
    1 ordinary white sewing thread No. 60
    1 spool ordinary black sewing thread No. 60
    1 paper of millinery needles No. 5
    1 paper of sharps No. 8 for fine work
    1 apron, 1 tape line, 1 notebook, 1 pencil
    1 pair of shears, 8 inches long
    1 pair smaller scissors, with sharp points
    1 wooden foot rule, 1 pair of millinery pliers
    1 paper of pins, 1 piece of white brace wire
    1 piece of black brace wire, 1 spool of black tie wire
    1 spool of white tire wire, 1 spool of uncovered tie wire

Other materials can be purchased as needed. It is well to keep a flat basket on the table, with all the tools of construction in it. A few aluminum thimbles are always a convenience, for it never pays to expend time in hunting anything. The spool rack, basket and pin tray should be kept on the table, and with the work on hand can be covered at night with a cloth. The remainder of the furnishings can be placed in the drawer of the table.

The work table should always be near a gas plate or stove, where a pressing iron can be heated or a tea kettle boiled for steam.

Millinery Thread

Millinery thread is specially prepared for the art of hat making. It is well twisted and heavily waxed so that it will glide through fabrics easily. It unwinds like wire and must always be caught in the slit of the spool.

Millinery Needles

No. 24 millinery thread requires a No. 5 millinery needle, and these are the sizes used in all the heavier parts of hat construction. The thread is made so strong in order that fewer stitches may be required, and the length of the needle is for reaching spaces that otherwise could not be covered.

Threading the Needle

When threading the needle, hold the thread taut between the thumb and fingers of the left hand and cut the thread on the bias. This gives it a point which be careful not to touch, and it will go through the eye of the needle without any trouble. If the thread is broken off, cut square or dampened, it will loosen the wax, fray and make it difficult to thread.

When finer thread is required, *never* use silk. Silk thread is an abomination to the milliner, although it sometimes has to be employed because a color cannot be matched in any cotton thread. When silk is used for gathering it frays out and breaks. A knot made of it is liable to slip. For the same reasons the mercerized cotton thread is not desirable. Get the fine, hard twisted cotton thread for fine work; it can be depended upon.

Millinery Wires

As to the wires, the ordinary frame or brace wire may be covered with silk or cotton, but never get that which is covered with paper or a slack, flimsy cotton covering that frays at sight. The wire must be firmly covered, to make a good frame. If the braid or fabric to be used in the construction of the hat is such that the frame will not show through, the uncovered tie wire can be used. But if it is transparent or has interstices that will reveal the frame, the tie wire must be covered to match the brace wire. Covered tie wire is never as strong as the uncovered, and consequently has to be used with greater care or it will break under the twisting of the pliers.

The Useful Notebook

Nothing is more useful than a notebook. There are constantly coming up items worth preserving, which if fastened to paper will stay with you, while otherwise they would vanish away.

Millinery Pliers

It is economy to buy the best millinery pliers and scissors. They should be of the best steel, as they last a lifetime. See that the tip of the plier will hold a tie wire, so that it can be twisted. Sometimes the wire cutter on the side of the blade holds the tip of the pliers apart, when they are almost useless for frame making.

With these preparations we are now ready for the first lesson.

When we build a house, we first assemble the material. The next thing requisite is to be able to use the tools. We will now build a wire frame, and to do so acquaint ourselves with the use of the millinery pliers. Hunt up an old wire hat frame, cut the wires, until you use the pliers with ease, and can make a clean cut without tearing out the covering of the wire (Figure 1). Next learn to catch the end of the wires with the pliers, and turn them down at right angles. Now take two pieces of wire and cross them, and put the wire around them

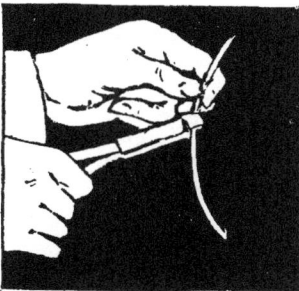

Figure 1
Cutting wire with pliers.

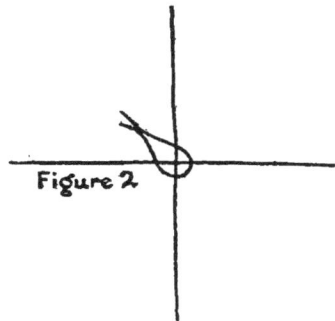

Figure 2

The wire placed around
intersection.

(Figure 2). Hold the two pieces of wire in the left hand, and manage the tie wire and pliers with the right. Twist the tie wire around the crossed wires (Figure 3), cut off the wire, leaving about one-quarter of an inch, which press down with the pliers.

The one-piece frame is much simpler than the two-piece frame. If the headsize of a one-piece frame fits as it should, the crown is necessarily not very large, and if fashion dictates a large crown the headsize must be correspondingly large, and a bandeau used to make it fit the head.

A frame is made of regular frame wire, either silk or cotton covered, but we designate the wires that run up and down and those that run around the frame by different names.

The wires that go around the frame on the outside and give its real shape are called stay wires. Those that proceed from the crown center to the brim edge are called brace wires, because they brace the stay wires in position. When the crown is separate the stay wires at the top and bottom are called respectively the crown top and the crown base. The outer stay

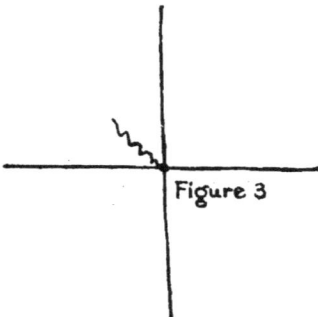

Tie wire twisted. To be cut
near intersection.

Figure 4
Placing the "head size" wire.

wire of the brim is called the edge wire, and the circle that comes next to the head is called the headsize. In a one-piece frame the headsize and the crown base are the same wire.

A COMPLETE COURSE IN MILLINERY

The One-Piece Frame

Cut four pieces of frame wire from a bolt, each 25 inches in length. It will be easiest to straighten out each 25 inches as you cut it. Hold the end of the wire in the left hand, letting the rest of it curve out and downward. Pass the wire through the right hand, with the thumb pressed hard between the first and second fingers, holding the fingers the least bit apart. Draw the wire through the fingers, pulling by the left hand, until it is straightened perfectly. Never try to do this by sudden bends along the wire's length, or it will be in notches. Take the four pieces of wire, form them into a bundle, side by side, tie them in the middle with the tie wire wrapped about them three or four times and twisted up, not too tightly, as the wires must now be spread out, as shown in Figure 5. Bend down each end one-half of an inch. At 4 inches from the tied center bend each wire downward at right angles to make the side crown. This should be 3½ inches long. Then bend the wires outward at right angles to form the brim. Take a wire 26 inches long and overlap it 2 inches and secure each end with tie wire. Slip this over the crown and secure to each brace wire at the head-size. Let the brace wires be equally distant from each other. (Figure 4). The overlapping wires denote the back of the frame. Make a second circle the same size as this first one and place it about the crown top, putting the overlap at the back. Cut a piece of wire 53 inches long, overlap the ends 2 inches, and fasten with tie wire. This is the edge wire. Place the circle within the downward turned ends of the brace wires, and press the brace wires firmly about the edge wire with the pliers. Let all overlaps be at the back. This gives the main structure of the frame, but it needs three more wire circles to complete it, one between the edge wire and the headsize, another on the side crown between the headsize and the crown top, and the

11

last between the crown top and the center of the crown. These three wires are secured with tie wire wherever they cross a brace wire. This completes a one-piece frame (Figure 6),

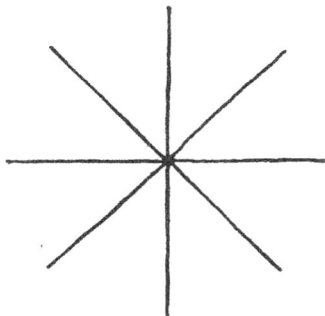

Figure 5—Brace wires tied with tie wire at center and spread apart.

Figure 6—Wire placed midway between wire and headsize.

which can be varied as to size or shape of brim or crown, as fancy may dictate.

A curved crown top and sloping side crown may be fashioned by making the first of the brace wires into the desired shape and forming the three others by the first.

In a like manner the brim may be made narrow or wide, drooping or turned up or given any fancy shape.

By practice one soon acquires the faculty of shaping a one-piece wire frame to meet any demand of fashion.

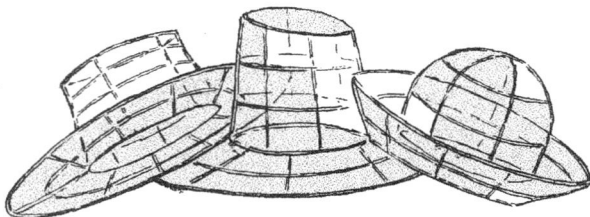

LESSON II

To Make a Two-Piece Wire Frame

The standard shape for a two-piece wire frame is the sailor, which can be modified and changed to almost any other form. We will first make a round, flat-topped crown with straight sides. Cut four pieces of wire each 16½ inches long. Put them side by side in a bundle, tie them in the centre with tie wire, then loosen up so they may be spread out as shown in Figure 5, in Lesson No. 1 (see page 12). Turn all the ends downward at right angles for a half inch; 4½ inches from the center, turn down the wires at right angles to form the side crown, which will be 3½ inches high. Take 27½ inches of wire, overlap it 2 inches, making a circle. Secure the ends with tie wire. Lay this circle over the turned-down ends of the brace wire, press the ends about the circle with the pliers, keeping the wires equally spaced. Then make a similar circle to place about the side crown where the top begins and let all overlaps be in the back. Put one more stay wire between the headsize, and the crown top and the center of the crown. Secure all

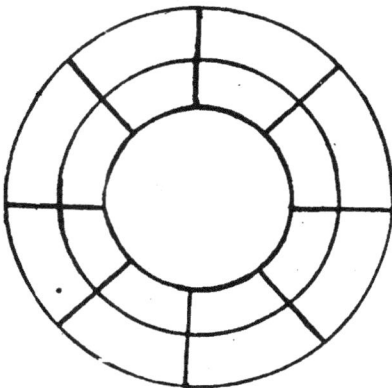

Figure 1—The circular brim. Figure 2—The elongated brim.

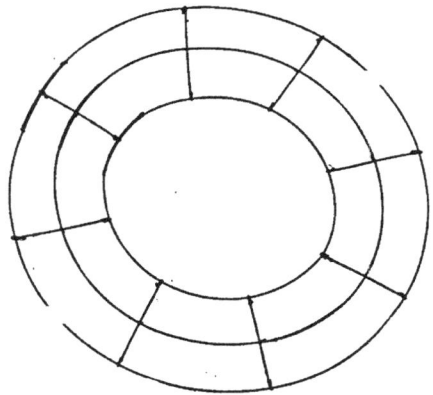

these with tie wires, allowing 2 inches overlap in each instance. This completes the crown. Cut a piece of wire 53 inches long and another 26½ inches long, overlap each 2 inches and fasten with tie wire. Make complete circles of each. Place the smaller one, which is the headsize, within the larger one, which is the edge wire. Have them equally distant from each other at all points. Measure the distance from the headsize to the edge wire and cut eight wires that length, plus 1 inch. This allows ½ inch at either end of these brace wires to turn over the headsize wire first and the edge wire. Put them all on the headsize wire first and then secure them to the edge wire, pressing them down firmly with the pliers. It is easier to space these wires by fastening first the wire in the back, which will come in the middle of the overlap of the headsize; then the one in front and next the two side ones. The four intervening wires are then easily placed. One more stay wire is needed between the headsize and the brim edge. This is put on the upper side of the brim and secured with tie wire. All overlays come in the back. (See Figures 1 and 2, page 13.)

Wiring the Brim

If the braid to be used is heavy or for any reason extra stability is desired, double wire the brim edge. This is done by cutting a wire the same length as the brim edge, placing it underneath the edge and wrapping the two wires together with thread. Take your needle, put a double thread in it, and knot the ends. Slip this knot over the two wires and pass your needle under the wires and between the threads just above the knot. Cinch it up and this gives a good anchorage for the start. Put the needle around and around the two wires, disposing the thread at even intervals. This makes a firm edge, and one that will hold any shape in which one desires to bend it. Remember in constructing a frame that the stay wires are always outside of the brace wires except on the edges, as the brace edge, or the headsize. This completes the two-piece frame

How the Brim May Be Varied

To vary this shape take the brim first. Make the headsize as before directed, fasten on the eight brace wires and bend them in any shape desired; next put them on the edge wire, fastening it to each of the eight wires in turn, all the while carefully preserving the desired shape. Close the edge wire last and then brace with one or two wires between the edge wire and the headsize. If one side is to turn up it may be necessary to cut some of the brace wires longer than others. If a drooping brim is affected the edge wire is simply contracted. Practice will soon make it easy to develop any shape the mind may suggest.

Varying the Crown

The crown is varied by taking a piece of wire and making the exact outline desired. Then cut four of these wires and allow ½ inch on each end to turn over the headsize wire. It may be a round crown or only rounding at the crown top, but there is no limit to the shapes it may assume. In an oblong crown the brace wires are shorter on the sides than from the front to the back. The headsize of any frame does not fit well when it is perfectly round. If the brim in Figure 1 is pulled from front to back, it will assume the shape shown in Figure 2, and can be made to fit any shaped head and not change the flat brim. The headsize of the brim is necessarily always a little smaller than the headsize of the crown, in order that the crown may set on the brim. An allowance should always be made in fitting the brim headsize for the braid or fabric of which it is made must turn up into the headsize and moreover there will be two thicknesses of the hat lining about the headsize. For that reason the headsize should be larger than the required size when finished. An average way to determine this is to insert two fingers under the wire, when placing it about the head to get the headsize. This will allow the right enlargement. When the brim headsize is oval, the head-size of the crown should correspond and an ng cr i the consequence as shown in Figure 3.

Figure 3—The round cro

Frames which are to be cover erials which are not transparent can be ma wire. But if they are of open work or ma trans-parent material, covered tie wire mpletes instruction on the wire frame.

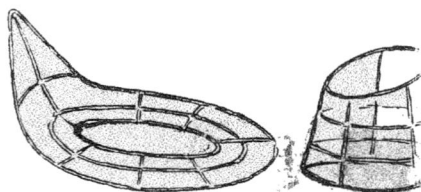

LESSON III

The Stitches Used in Millinery

Now, as our wire frame is completed, we will learn some of the stitches we must use, in covering the frame, and in subsequent lessons on millinery.

The simplest is the running stitches, shown in Figure 1 in shirrings or gatherings. The stitches can be run on the needle, until it is full, before it is drawn through the fabric is light and thin. There is

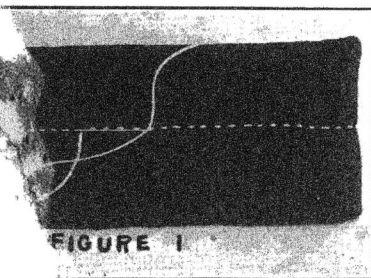

Running Stitch

never two thicknesses of cloth used in gathering.

shows the back stitch, which is used in sewing

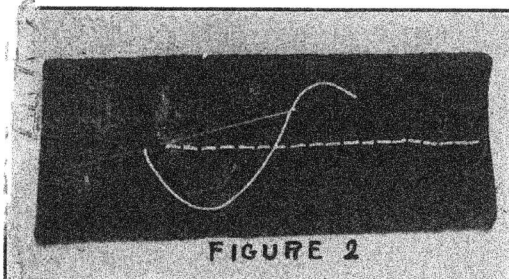

Drop Stitch

17

two thicknesses of fabric together in a seam. In sewing together strips of velvet or cloth, or anything that requires a
stout seam, the back stitch is most efficient. The first stitch
is taken the same as the running stitch; it is pulled clear
through, and the next stitch, thrust in, at the middle of the
fabric, taken up by the first stitch, and completed the same distance in *front* of the termination of the first stitch, as the beginning of the second stitch is *behind it*. This repeated, m'ing
each stitch back of the last one, gives us the process of back
stitching.

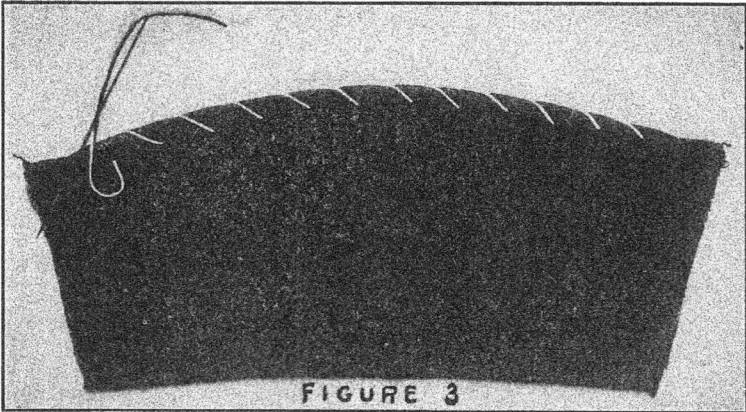

Overcast Stitch

Figure 3 is the overcast stitch, and is used to join selvage
edges, or to overcast the edge of brims or crown base. The
stitch is made by throwing or casting the thread over an edge,
and drawing the needle through, always in the same direction.
In gathering laces and very light materials the overcast stitch
is often used.

Figure 4 shows the feather stitch. It is used to hold down
a hem, or for ornamentation. It is really made by sewing backward, and runs toward the right, while all others run toward

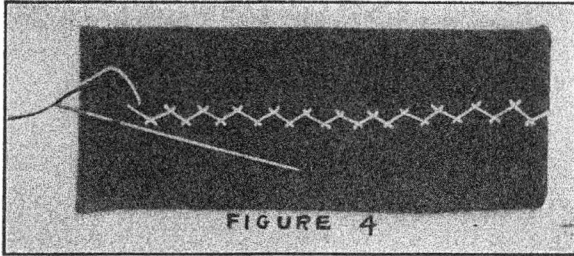

Feather Stitch

the left. At the extreme left of your hem, or row of ornamental work take one running stitch toward the left and draw it clear through. Move toward the right at an angle of 45 degrees, and take another running stitch toward the left. The third stitch is made at the same angle toward the right, but we swing back on a straight line from the first stitch, and so it goes on, swinging from side to side, and progressing to the right all the time.

The feather stitch is used to sew ribbon wire to ribbons, and the edges of flat seams are often secured by it. In fancy work it is one of the most ornamental stitches.

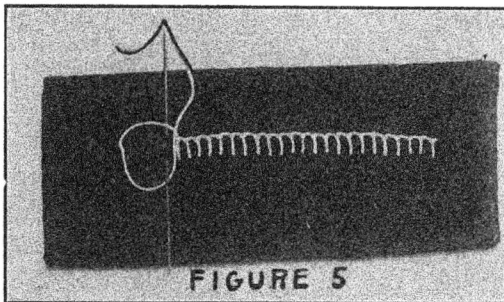

Buttonhole Stitch

The buttonhole stitch, shown in Figure 5, is used to finish edges, secure wires, or as a finishing stitch to fasten the end of

19

thread. It is employed in appliqué work. For buttonholes the stitches are placed close together, making a firm edge.

The slip stitch is one of the most important and the stitch most frequently used in millinery work. Its main object is to lay a flat hem without turning under the last edge, thus making only two thicknesses of the goods, instead of three. Take up the least possible threads, with the needle on the back of the goods, then slip the needle under the raw edge that is turned over for the hem, and·let it be quite a distance from this edge, where the needle comes through, so it will not pull out. Then again, take a second small stitch and thrust through upper flap again, as shown in Figure 6. If this is properly done, it will not show the stitches on the right side at all in velvet and very little in other fabrics.

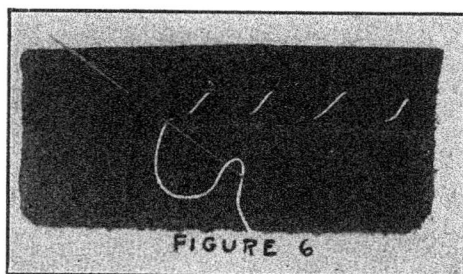

Slip Stitch

The blind stitch, Figure 7, is used where we want no stitch to show at all on either side. The sample shows two edges brought together with this stitch, so all the thread will disappear from view when it is drawn up tight. Insert the needle in the tube-like edge of the fold, take the length of a good sized stitch and bring the needle out just under the edge of the fold. Exactly opposite, insert it in the other fold, on its edge, take the same length stitch and bring across to the needle in the same manner as the first stitch. Take the needle across to the fold opposite in a straight line, and insert again. Repeat this process and draw the edges together as you go. If the thread is not taken across from one fold to the other in a *straight* line, but is allowed to *slant,* it cannot be pulled tight enough to cause the thread to disappear. Remember this point, for it is the frequent mistake of blind-stitching. This stitch can be used for a hem by taking up the smallest portion of the fabric just even with the turned under edge of the hem, draw the needle through and exactly opposite on the hem itself insert the needle on the edge and let it slide along in the tube-like roll of the goods, the length of a good-sized stitch and bring out on the

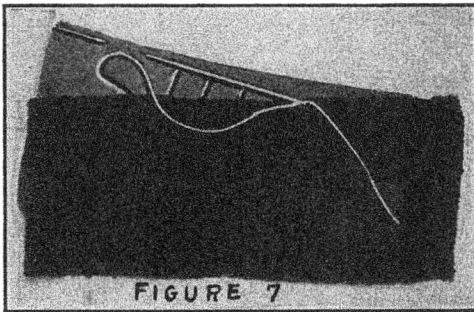
Blind Stitch

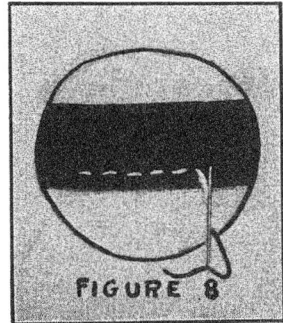
Stab Stitch

edge of the hem, and opposite it on the fabric take another tiny stitch, cinch it up and all the thread will disappear. The blind stitch is used not only for hems but for putting in facings for brims, making rolled edges and drawing together the turned in edges of velvet hat brims. In the latter case the stitches can be made of the same length as the edges are brought together.

The stab stitch, Figure 8, is only used in sewing a heavy fabric, such as buckram, or when sewing on trimmings. The needle goes clear through, the thread following, and then back in the same manner, both strokes being required to make the one stitch.

21

The saddlers' stitch, Figure 9, is used for making folds holding together turned-in edges to make a seam. The needle is passed through the edge as in the slip stitch, and then through

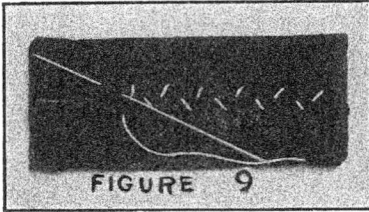

FIGURE 9

Saddler's Stitch

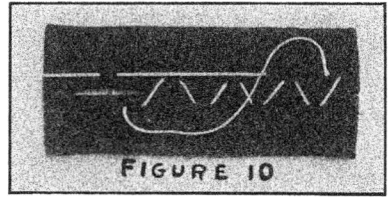

FIGURE 10

Lacing Stitch

the opposite edge the same way. Go back and forth in this manner, sewing toward the left and each stitch advancing in that direction at an angle of 45 degrees.

The lacing stitch, Figure 10, is used exactly as the saddlers' stitch, and is made like it, only a small running stitch is taken up on either edge, instead of a slip stitch.

The tie stitch, Figure 11, is used for putting on trimming

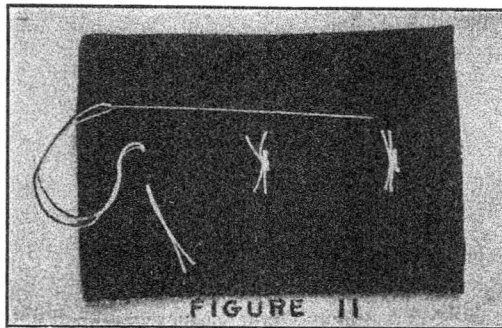

FIGURE 11

Tie Stitch.

or securing loops of ribbon, or for any purpose which needs but the one stitch. A hat is seldom finished without use of a tie stitch. It may be used to secure a leaf, flower, fold or lining, and the crown is often fastened to the brim by tie stitches only. It is made by passing the needle through and back again as in the stab stitch, tying it twice and cutting off short. If great strength is desired, use double thread.

The hidden stitch, Figure 12, is used when a hat crown is sewed on to the brim. Whether the tie stitch or the stilting stitch is employed it must come through the fabric of the brim, where a stitch is most undesirable. If the thread, usually double, is brought through on the under brim, if it be firmly pulled to the right, it will make a tiny opening in the fabric where the needle first came through, and while the thread is held very taut, insert the point of the needle in the tiny hole at the thread base, incline the needle at a different angle from which it came through in the first place, and when the thread is drawn back through the hole it will disappear entirely if no portion of the fabric has been allowed to come between the thread base and the needle point. If the threads of the goods are slightly disarranged they can easily be put in place by the needle point.

The stilting stitch (Figure 13) is used in sewing brim edges together or in sewing the braid on the upper side of a

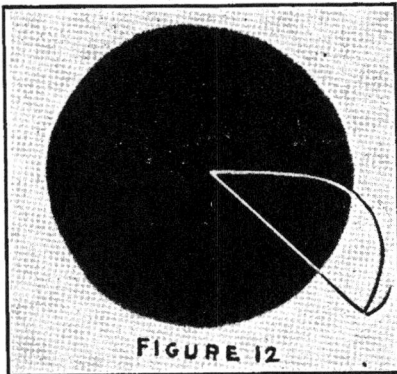

FIGURE 12

Hidden Stitch

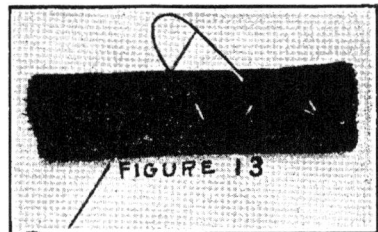

FIGURE 13

Stilting Stitch

A concealed stitch very much used in millinery work

23

hat brim, where the needle necessarily passes through the braid on the lower side of the brim, and the stitching must be concealed on both sides. The stitch is made by inclining the needle at an angle of 5 degrees and sewing back and forth toward the left at this angle, as shown in the sample. The least possible thread is visible. The needle is supposed to take the posture of a boy walking on stilts, hence its name.

The sliding stitch (Figure 14) is simply a loop of the thread, slid along by the needle and drawn into a knot. It is used where it is impossible to take a stitch and the only way to fasten the thread is to slide this loop along and secure with its knot. It is particularly useful where the hat lining is drawn together.

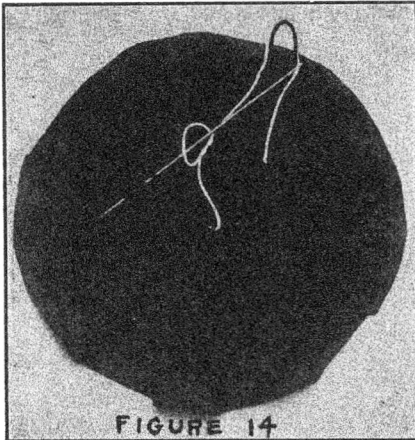

Sliding Stitch

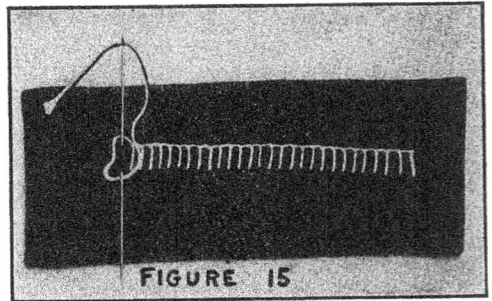

Blanket Stitch

The blanket stitch (Figure 15) is exactly like the buttonhole stitch, except that the thread is thrown over the point of the needle from left to right, while in the buttonhole stitch the thread is thrown from right to left. The blanket stitch makes a softer edge than the buttonhole stitch and is more desirable in most millinery work.

24

LESSON IV

To Cover a Wire Frame

We will now take our two-piece wire frame and cover it with mull or crinoline for a foundation upon which to sew the braid. If the braid to be used covers well, crinoline is the better of the two, as it is a little stiffer than mull, but if the interlining will show through, mull will look better than the crinoline. Some of the fancy straws and hair braids have such wide interstices that it is often best to cover the frame with a cheap mercerized lining fabric that looks like silk, and has as much body to it. This generally matches the straw in color, and is usually used on the upper side of the brim and the outside of the crown. Transparent hats of chiffon, lace and maline are made differently and will be considered later. Whatever interlining is chosen, place the front of the brim in a bias corner of the goods and let it lie smoothly over the upper side of the brim. Secure by turning the goods over the brim edge and pinning it there. First

No. 1 Crown frame partly covered

put in a pin, on the straight of the goods at right angles, and its opposite. This leaves the four bias places between, where all wrinkles can be taken out. Put in the pins about an inch

25

apart, being careful not to pull the goods, so as to cramp the brim or change its shape.

Cut off the surplus goods, leaving ⅓ inch overlap around the brim edge. Oevrcast it as shown in the picture. Then cut the headsize, leaving about ¾ of an inch to sash, and turn over the headsize wire. Overcast the same as the brim edge. This is clearly shown in the diagram. Next the crown must be covered. If the top is flat, cover the same as the brim; that is, place the front on a bias of the goods, and pin it first on the straight of the goods, and then on its opposite, next on the straight, at right angles, and then on its opposite, and then secure the four bias pieces between. Use pins one inch

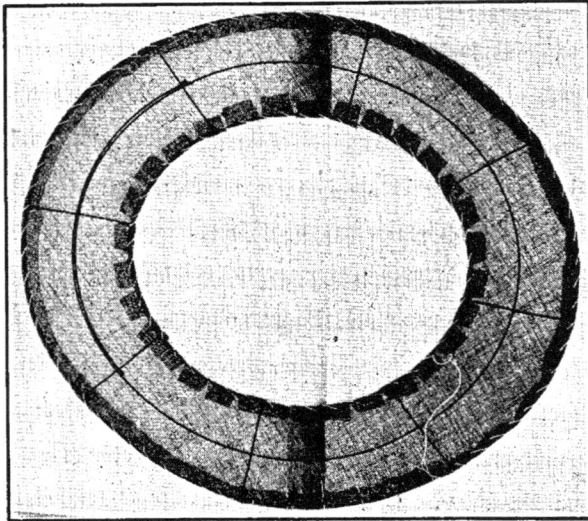

No. 2 Crinoline—covered wire brim

apart and cut away the goods, leaving ⅓ of an inch over the outer wire of the crown top. Overcast this as shown in illustration. The reason for pinning the interlining on the straight of the goods first is that it cannot pull out of shape, across it, or in its length; but on the bias it can always be pulled into another form. If the top of the crown is round-ing, the fulness can sometimes be taken up by pulling and smoothing down the bias places in the goods, or the covering may be slit, as shown in the picture, lapped over and stitched up until the parts will not hold the thread, when you must change to a lock stitch, across the seam, as shown in the sample, near the crown top. If this fulness is laid over in plaits it will be found very hard to manage and get smooth, as it nears the center of the crown. Next cut a piece of the goods long enough to go around the side crown and to overlap one inch. Let it be also one inch wider than the side crown is high. Turn in half inch on the edge, which goes next to the crown top and pin it around the side crown, just even with the outer wire of the crown top. Lap it over the extra inch, allowed in measuring around the side crown and sew it together with long stab stitches. Sew the side crown on next to the crown top, with long stitches on the right side, as shown in diagram. At the headsize turn under the goods, pin it and overcast. The frame is now ready for the braid.

We will next consider the covering of wire shapes that may be varied from the sailor. As mull is more pliant than crinoline, it is better for these irregular forms. If the crown is round or bell shaped, it is sometimes covered with one piece. This can be done when the braid will not show through. Place a straight piece of the mull at the front of the crown, turn it under at the headsize and pin. Then pin the goods, at right angles to the front. Now drape down the opposite side similarly; next the two straight places in all the fulness possible at the four bias places, between the

27

four straight points that are pinned, and form each bias place into five plaits, all turning the same way.

This takes up the fulness. Another way is to slash the bias places and lay one fold of the goods over the other, as in the sailor crown top. This is more apt to ravel. A third method is to cut out small gores and then overlap. In any case, the crown is overcast at the headsize after it is pinned and the fulness disposed of. Suppose the brim is turned up all around, as in some turban shapes. Then the mull is placed on the under side, next to the face. The bias is put to the front, and pinned in the four straight places of the goods. What fulness can be taken up by stretching is disposed of, and if more remains it is plaited over, slashed and overlaid, or a gore taken out. Then overcast around the brim edge, and manage the headsize, as in the sailor. In fluted brims, or those that flare much, it is often necessary to insert a gusset wherever needed. Many milliners prefer to cut out plaques for covering the frames before beginning the process. In that case measurements must be taken from front to back and from side to side and a plaque cut out large enough to cover and allow an inch extra. The only difficulty in this method is that the plaque will stretch so much on the bias that its form is changed more or less and the goods may come short at one point and have to be cut away at others. It is not so economical as when pinned from the whole piece of goods. These varied forms can be covered with crinoline, only it takes a little more care and management, but with practice any frame can be smoothly covered.

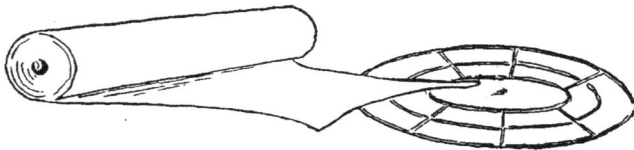

LESSON V

Applying the Covering to Hat Foundation

We now have the wire frame, made and covered with crinoline or mull, and will proceed to sew on the braid. Sometimes it is fashionable to bind the brim edge with the braid. If the braid is straw, turn in ½ inch on the end. If it is lace, or hair braid, tie the end and turn it in. Begin on the brim edge, in the back, and let the braid extend equally, on both sides of the brim edge. Sew it around, near the edge of the braid, back and forth, with a stab stitch, about ½ inch long, on either side. When the braid comes around to the place of beginning, turn it under on the end and bring the first and second ends together flat and sew them down. The first row of braid is sewed on the under side of the brim. Begin in the back, at the point where the binding began. Turn in the end of the braid if it is quite wide, and let the edge o fit project over the brim edge, stitching just within the brim edge wire, with the small stitch, on the under part of the brim, and the long one, on its top. Stitches ½ inch apart will hold it nicely. When the complete circle of the brim is made, end it by turning in the braid for ½ inch and sewing the two ends down flat. Then stitch the edge of the braid, nearest the headsize, with long stitches on the under side of the brim, and short ones on the upper. Whenever silks, velvets or braids are to be held in place, and the stitching will not eventually show, the long stitch is put on the right side, because it does more toward holding the fabric in place. For instance, this row of braid is sewed with the small stitch on its outer edge, because it will show, and the long stitch on its inner edge, because it wants to be held firmly and will be covered with the next row of braid.

The second row of braid starts in the back, is turned under,. and stitched down, with the edge nearest the brim edge, overlapping the first row of braid sufficiently to hide the stitches on its inner edge.

Sew it on with the small stitch, on the right side, and the long stitch on the wrong or upper brim side, making the sewing come, as nearly as possible directly above the stitching, on the inner edge of the first row; when around, finish it the same as the first row. Continue this process until the under-brim is completed to the headsize. If the last row is too wide, let it extend up into the headsize, for the headsize wire must always be covered with the braid, and it must extend up into the crown far enough to be stitched to the braid that extends from the upper side of the brim and held in an upright position toward the crown top. This makes a foundation to sew the crown lining to. If one side of the brim is wider than the other or the brim is of irregular shape, the last row of braid will have a bare space near the headsize. Fill this in, with short lengths of braid, overlapped like the outer circles, and let the ends extend up into the headsize.

The upper side of the brim is sewed on exactly the same as the lower one, only the stilting stitch is used, so it will not show on either side. As either the upper or lower side of the brim must be sewed through, in order to get the braid on both sides, it is best to sew *through* the under side, so there will be the least sewing on the upper side. If the braid is one inch or under in width it can be laid on flat at the beginning instead of turning under the end, and when the circle is sewed around it can be gradually sloped toward the headsize until it comes to the regular overlapping width desired, and from that point it will go around row after row as shown in the picture. When the brim edge is not bound

with the braid it is finished by sewing together the projecting edges of the braid from above and underneath. The
stilting stitch is used in small stitches. This makes a neat
finish. If a braid is stiff and brittle, steam will soften it, or
wrapping it about with a wet bath towel, wrung out as dry
as possible.

If the braid is colored in light hues and may run with
moisture, put a dry cloth about the braid first, then wrap the
damp towel around it, and let it lie a while before using. In
high altitudes it is sometimes necessary to dip the braid in
water.

There is no rule laid down by a milliner but what can
be modified and changed, so as to give great variety. Take

Crown foundation,
covered

When the crown and the brim
have been finished separately,
they are sewed together in place

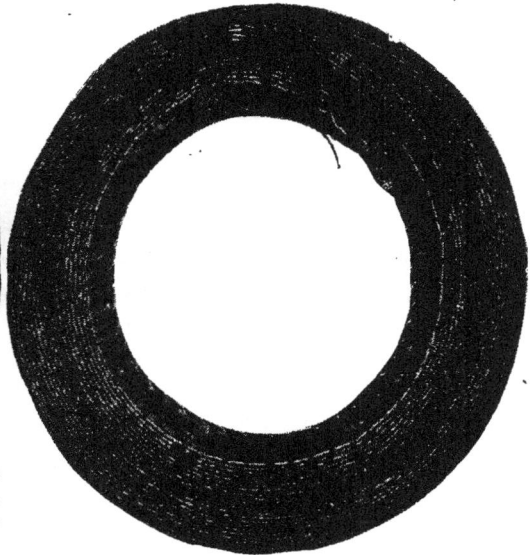

Brim section of frame, after
braid is applied

the brim edge as an example. It may be finished by bringing
together the braid from above and below, or it can be bound
with the braid of the hat, or with silk or velvet, which might

31

be in the color of the braid, or the hue of the trimming. In each case the looks and general expression would be entirely different.

Covering the Crown

We will now consider the crown. To cover a bell shaped crown, it is easiest to begin in the back at the headsize. Let the finished edge of the braid be down and slope it gradually from underneath the headsize wire until the lower edge of the braid lays smoothly along the headsize wire.

Then go round and round toward the crown top, sewing the lower edge of the braid first with the small stitch on the right side and the long one on the wrong side. The upper edge of the braid is sewed on with the long stitch on the right side. When the crown tip is reached, the braid is brought around in a complete circle, and applied so it makes a round rosette for a finish, as shown in the illustration. Stitch this finishing rosette down very smoothly. In hair braid and some of the soft straws this finishing circle can be made by drawing up the braid on its gathering string, but if the braid is stiff it has to be formed by laying it in plaits, all coming to a common center.

If the crown is straight on the sides and flat or rounding on top, sew the top crown first, starting in the back, at the crown top edge, and letting the braid project about ¼ inch over this crown top edge. When once around, slope the braid gradually into the second circle, as in brim sewing, and finish with the rosette at the crown top. This rosette is never separate, but is a continuation of the braid until it curls around on itself. Next begin on the side crown at the back next to the crown top edge. Let the finished edge of the braid be up and project ¼ of an inch above the crown top edge. There it will meet the finished edge from the top of the crown, and these edges are in contact, extending outward in a little ridge, and are stitched together with small stilting stitches. When the first circle about the side crown is completed, gradually slope the braid down until its finished edge covers the stitching on the lower edge of the first row. Proceed row on row in the same manner until the braid is run under at the headsize.

The crown is now sewed on the brim, with long stilting stitches that do not show on either side, and the hat is complete. Some use a tie stitch in putting on a crown, but unless there is a fold or trimming to go about the crown base these stitches are not desirable. It takes about 8 stitches of this kind to secure the crown to the brim.

In sewing any kind of braid on a curve the finished or outer edge is slightly stretched, and the inner or plain edge is drawn up on the gathering thread so it will lie smooth and natural. All the braid must be placed and pinned before sewing. Next lesson will be on fancy ways of sewing braids.

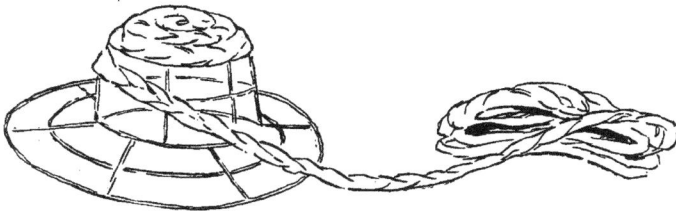

LESSON VI

Sewing Braid in Fancy Forms

After learning to sew the braid on the frame smoothly it is well to have some variations of its use, as there is a vast field open to imaginative genius in inventing beautiful and decorative forms for the use of braid. For this purpose a pliable braid is the best, although a stiff braid, by the aid of

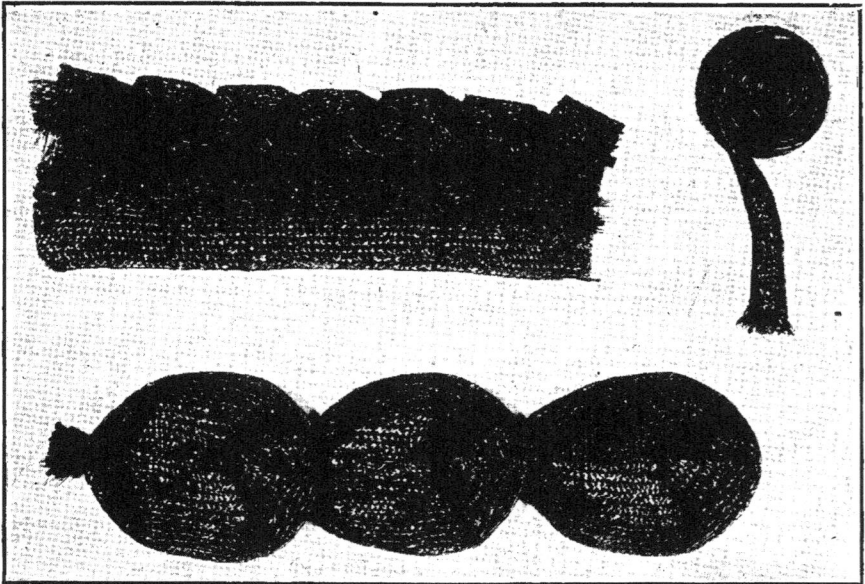

Various ways of using straw braid ornamentally

steam, or moisture, from being wrapped in a damp cloth, can be made to assume various forms; also hair braid is particularly fine, for round swirls, being drawn up on the gathering string, on the plain edge. But for general purposes a medium braid is preferable, neither so stiff as some straws nor so lacy as hair braid. The braid we choose must have a gathering string, or if it has not one must be run in its plain edge, before making the swirls. '

Straw Leaves

The first form to consider is that of straw leaves, as shown in the picture. Take the end of the braid for the stem of the leaf. Double over a plait, toward the stem, letting it bag out a little; never pull it straight. Leave a plain piece of the braid, about its own width; then make another plait, diagonally across the braid, leave another space, the width of the braid, and form another plait, whose inner base shall come exactly to the inner base of the plait just before it. This last plait will stand straight with the midrib of the leaf. Leave another space, the width of the braid, and form another plait diagonally, and whose inner base will come to the other two. The depth of these plaits must be determined by the width of the braid, and will be so formed that the top of the leaf will lie flat, and the inner edge of the braid going down to the stem again, will overlap the inner edge of the braid, as it went up to form the top of the leaf. This stitched together forms the midrib of the leaf, a last plait is taken at the base, like the first one, only opposite, each of them drawing in toward the stem; stitch this last plait and wrap the thread around the raw ends several times and the leaf is finished.

These leaves may be used around the crown at the headsize, sewed as shown in the illustration, or stood upright, one after another, and their base covered with a folded or plaited braid. They can be sewed in a' circle on the top of a crown or used to ornament the brim. Fancy can suggest multitudinous forms for their use. When sewing them on be careful not to lose the expression by sewing them down too flat; yet they must be secure.

If a brim is smaller than desired, a plaited edge adds to its size and embellishes its looks. In the picture are two designs—the side plait and the box plait. They are stitched under the braid at the upper brim edge, and then the braid from the under side can be fastened with a stilting stitch, sewing through and through. These plaits can be used to decorate the crown edge, or by putting them on each side of a braid, a band for the base of the crown is formed for a trimming effect. Cabochons can be made by sewing these plaits around and around a disk, using the tight curled cabochon for a center. Many pretty effects can be studied out along the line of cabochons. The one shown in the picture is made by doubling the braid and curling it around on itself, sewing it through and through on the under side and the end, finally taken gradually down underneath, then by pushing the center up from the under side it gives it a slightly curved appearance. Cabochons are used at the base or fastening end of feathers, or loops of ribbon, or for purely decorative purposes of their own. They are sometimes made small and used in rows, like buttons, giving a tailored effect.

Another Pleasing Use for Braid

Braid is sometimes sewed, with the edges raised up, and stitched together in a ridge instead of overlapping like shingles on a roof. This is shown in the picture and is particularly nice to give the lights and shadows of a braid. It is best in sewing it on a hat to baste down each row as you go to the place desired. It will not do to try to sew the edges together, and sew through the hat to place the braid at the same time. It destroys the effect. The basting should be done just below the ridge and a very little way from it. This particular sewing can be made in one piece and stretched over a crown top, where it shows its full beauty.

Braid can be sewed in circular form by lapping it around a pencil lengthwise and stitching together the edges with the saddler's stitch. If the pencil proves too small for the width of the braid, take a round stick of the proper diameter and just so the edges of the braid will come together for stitching. A wire can be run into this circular braid and it can then be bent into the shape of quills and it makes a fancy trim, fastened with a corresponding cabochon. It can be used in rows around the crown base for a band, or if a cord is drawn through it it can be curved into all manner of shapes for all manner of decorations.

The swirls, made by pulling up the drawstring tight and

Various ways of using straw braid ornamentally

having the outer edge so it will lie smooth, are made in one continuous piece by bringing the braid over on itself and going on to the formation of the next circle, after the first is completed. See the sample in the illustration. Hair braid takes especially well to this treatment. It makes beautiful side crowns and can be used on the brim also.

There is no end to the different forms that braid can be manipulated into by simply keeping your eyes open to the beauties of nature and the devices of men, found all about us in the every day world.

LESSON VII

Lining the Crown

After making the wire frame, covering it with crinoline or mull, and sewing on the braid, in plain rows, or fancy shapes, we come to a very mooted question in millinery. It is this: Shall the crown be lined before the trimming is put on or not? The best of milliners can be found contending warmly on either side of this subject. One says: Line the crown before trimming the hat, because it is apt to crush the bows of ribbon, or muss up the flowers if it is done afterward. The other side says: If the lining is put in first it is fre-

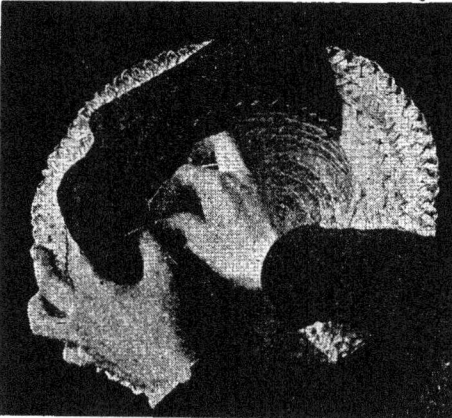

Figure No. 1

Lining Sewed in

with

Overcast Stitch

quently stitched through, in spite of all care, and is a constant aggravation. Whichever way you may choose you will probably wish you had tried the other. As a sort of compromise, some milliners put in the lining first, and then fold it into as tight a roll as possible, beginning at the raw upper edge, and pinning it, to confine the roll while trimming. Like most compromises, it has the virtue of neither side.

The present lesson will be on putting in the lining, and you can trim before or after it is placed, as you please. Personally, I prefer putting in the lining after trimming.

Materials for Hat Linings

The lining is made of different fabrics, according to the style and material of the hat. Light, soft silk makes the best lining, while many of the mercerized cotton fabrics made especially for this purpose are good for commoner use. For transparent hats, as chiffon, lace, maline or net, we line either with the same material as the hat, or something equally thin and delicate.

The lining may be cut lengthwise, in which case it will not ravel so easily, or crosswise, or bias.' Measure the headsize and allow two extra inches for the length of the lining, as it will take up a little of the fulness by sewing, be one ever so careful. Its width is from the headsize to the inside center of the crown. Ast he lower edge of the lining is sewed around the headsize and the upper edge is turned in to hold a draw ribbon, considerable material is taken from the width of the lining; so much so that a spot at the inner crown center would be left bare. So cut a piece of the lining fabric 4 inches square, place its middle directly over the inner center of the crown, sew it around its edge, taking long stitches on the inside of the crown, and very short ones on the outside. The piece of goods is called the crown tip, and in stores bears the name of the house or firm.

How to Adjust the Lining

Take the side lining in the long piece and turn in one edge half inch for a hem. Run a thread along it, 'leaving space for a tiny ribbon by which to draw it up. Fold one end of the lining in for half inch. Let it be folded over on the same side of the material as the hem was. Put this end fold exactly in the back of the crown at the headsize, with the raw edge of the lining length, extending into the crown. Sew from right to left, continuing around to the place of beginning. Hold the lining smooth, but do not draw it too tight. Two different stitches are used for this purpose. The first is shown in illustration No. 1, the overcast stitch. Remember this stitching must be done on the wrong side of the goods, and the top hem for the ribbon must be turned down on this side, too. Then when the lining is turned up into the crown, the right

Figure No. 2

Sewing in Lining

with

Buttonhole Stitch

side is exposed. The second stitch used in putting in a lining (illustration No. 2) is the buttonhole stitch. The overcast stitch is liable to show when the lining is turned up inside of the crown, as the material sometimes slips on the thread, but the buttonhole stitch, when drawn firmly outward, forms a continuous thread, to turn the lining over and is preferable for that reason.

To finish the lining tuck the last end under the folded end, sew firmly to place and baste the two ends together by taking a long stitch on the under side and the smallest possible one on the right side, and as near the edge of the turned under will be inserted. Run the ribbon through this hem with a metal runner, beginning at the lapped over end, and when it end as will hold. Continue this to the hem, where the ribbon comes around to the same point again thrust it through the goods on the right side, so it can be tied in a pretty bow; Fasten it to the crown top, with a tie stitch under the bow, and another tie stitch directly opposite it in the circle which the side lining will form, exposing the crown tip.

In cases where the smallest stitch will show on the top of the crown, make the lining wide enough to gather in a tight knob at the top, over which place a small flat bow of narrow ribbon. The top of the lining is folded in for half inch and the stitching done along the edge at the place of folding. Take a long stitch on the right side, and a small one on the wrong side, and when it is drawn tight it throws the fulness inside and leaves no aperture at all.

When the lining is sewed about the headsize before the trimming is placed, the upper edge of the lining must be left open until the trimming is done and then closed the last thing.

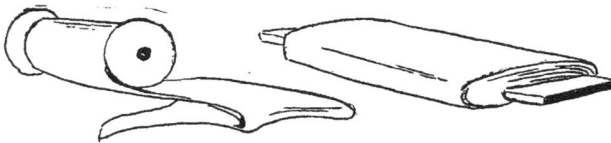

LESSON VIII

Making Hat Bandeaux

In order that a hat may stay on the head at a cartain angle, or to reduce the headsize or increase it, a bandeau must be uséd. The word bandeau means a band or fillet around a cap. So it defined the headsize of the cap, and consequently can be applied to the headsize of a hat, as a hat is merely a cap with a brim to it.

A bandeau is made on a buckram foundation. Never use rice net or any of the more pliable fabrics, as they are unsatisfactory. The buckram is wired all around as shown in Figure 1. The next step is to sew the wire beginning in the middle of the top, with an overcast stitch, keeping the wire even with the buckram edge, and allowing the ends to overlap about an inch, bringing the finishing end under the end of beginning. Use the usual No. 5 millinery needle and strong millinery thread. These foundations are made of various shapes to produce different effects. It may be a straight strip, all around the headsize, merely lifting the hat up from the head. Sometimes a bandeau is cut perfectly round, as shown in Figure 5, and is then called a halo. This is used to reduce the headsize. The halo has to be used when the crowns are very large, and the headsize so proportioned that it would let the head clear into the crown top of the hat.

A halo is sometimes basted in, against the side crown, to keep the head from coming too far into the hat. The sides of the halo may be slanting, instead of lying flat, in which case it fits the head better, and keeps the hat more firmly in place. The sloping effect can be accomplished by slitting the buckram from its outer circle almost through to the inner one, and

43

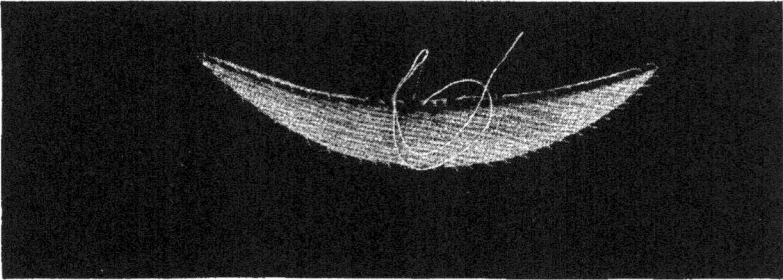

Figure 1. Bandeau stiffened with wire

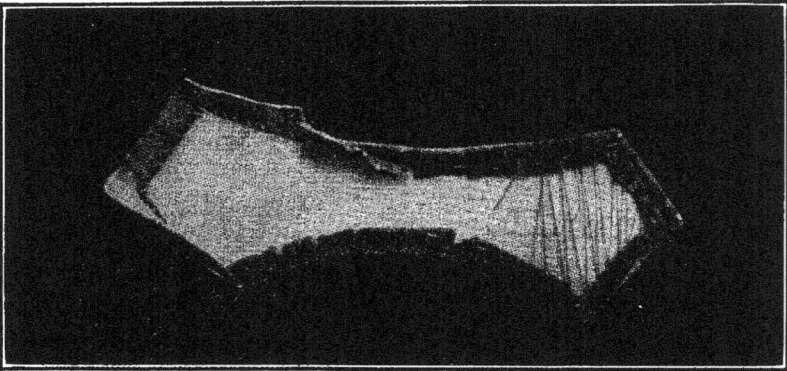

Figure 2. How edges of velvet are drawn with long stitches

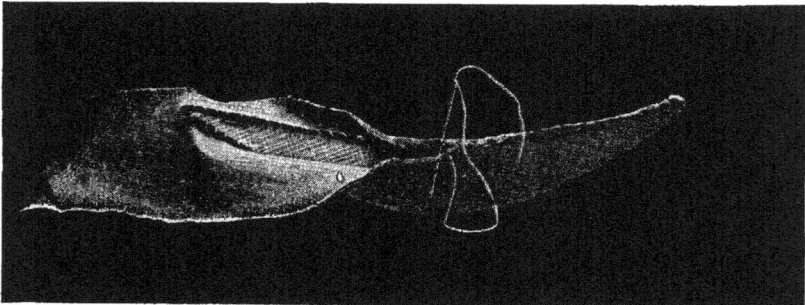

Figure 3. Bandeau covered with bias strip ·

overlapping the outer edges to get the required slant. Or a paper pattern can be cut of a halo, and treated in the same manner, and then cut across it, so it will lay out flat. Use this for a pattern for the buckram, thus making it in one continuous piece.

If a bandeau is to tilt the hat at an angle, it is put on either side, or at the front or back. Generally, if any direction is required, it is a tilt from the left side, and a trimming of flowers or ribbon covers the bandeau. The comfort of a hat depends upon the fit of the headsize. If it presses on the forehead, or any angle sticks into the head, it is almost unbearable. To obviate this, it is better to fit all bandeaux. Put the hat on the head, find its proper position, whether it needs to be tilted, brought up higher, or pulled down. Then take a finger and slip it about the headsize where the bandeau will be placed, and by gauging on the finger the distance from the headsize of the hat to the line where the lower edge of the bandeau will come, you can estimate the shape of the bandeau itself, and cut a stiff paper pattern as nearly the required form as possible. Leave an extra inch at the top of the pattern, and pin this extra inch within the headsize. This paper can be fitted by insets or overlaps so it will press evenly everywhere, and then the buckram can be cut by this pattern.

By curving the upper edge of the side bandeau so it is concave it can be made to flare out, more or less, as desired. Sew the wire on the rough side of the buckram, and let this side be away from the head, so the wires cannot be felt. To cover a bandeau, baste velvet on the rough side of the buckram and let it extend one-third of an inch beyond the edges as is demonstrated in the illustration (Figure 2). Draw the edges together by long stitches, sewed back and forth, as in Figure 2. Next remove the bastings. Always cover the outside, which is the rough side, with the velvet first, then

45

baste a bias piece across the inside. Cut it off around the edge, letting the end project about one-third of an inch. Turn in the edges, and blindstitch it on. This forms the lining of the bandeau. In covering such a bandeau as is shown in Figure 2 it is often necessary to slash the goods to make it fit, and in some cases the goods will lay over in plaits, and when this occurs, it is best to cut out a gore to make it lay smooth.

The more regular bandeau can be covered with a bias strip, twice as wide as the widest part of the buckram foundation, and allow half inch beside, to turn in the two edges, as shown in Figure 3. Fold the velvet about the buckram and beginning at one corner, fit it carefully, and cut away all unnecessary velvet except the quarter of an inch to turn in on either edge. Bring both edges together after they are turned in, and overcast them together, so that the seam will come on the outside, as it will be ridgy, like a rope, and should be next to the head. It is shown in Figure 3.

Sometimes the bandeau is cut from the buckram with a continuous piece, going up into the headsize, as Figure 4. This

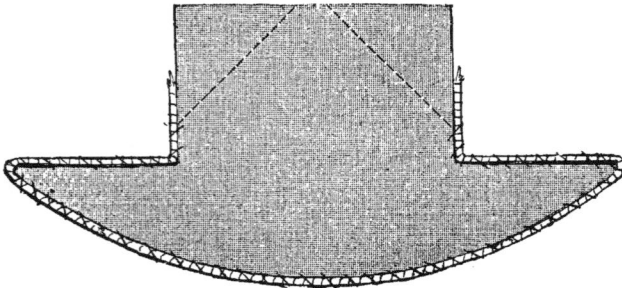

Figure 4. Bandeau with tab extension

extension is not wired or covered, but runs up into the crown to stiffen it for the trimming. If the hat is of soft substance, as hair braid, chiffon or lace, such support is necessary, and should be shaped so that the trimming will cover it.*

46

Figure 4 shows by dotted lines one of the many ways in which it may be cut off, and then basted to the crown. The bandeau part is covered with velvet or some fabric. ,

If a halo is flat it may be covered by placing the buckram foundation on a flat piece of velvet, basting it down and cutting the velvet around the outer edge, leaving quarter of an inch projection for a turn-in. Cut out the headsize, leaving quarter of an inch beyond the edge of the buckram. The two

Figure 5. The halo bandeau

edges are held in place by stitching back and forth, as in Figure 2, and need not be lined. The halo is shown in Figure 5.

There is one other kind of bandeau which is used in the back of a hat, to extend down on either side of the knot of back hair. It is used to hold flowers or some decoration.

Soft bandeaux are made from narrow strips of hat lining, sewed around the headsize and finished at the top with a hem through which a ribbon is drawn. By loosening or tightening the ribbon, the head is let more or less into the crown. If it is a, matter of reducing the headsize, however, the soft bandeau is not satisfactory, as it leaves the head so it will move all about, while at the same time it may be securely pinned to the hair.

LESSON IX

Making Buckram Frames

The standard shape for a buckram frame is a Gainsborough, and one having mastered its construction **can** easily learn to vary it to other shapes.

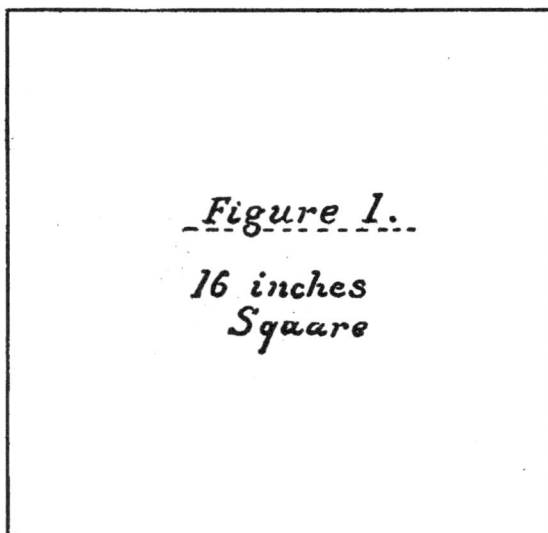

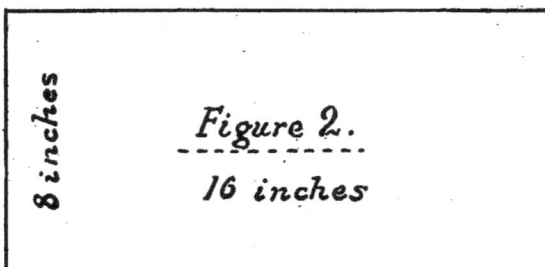

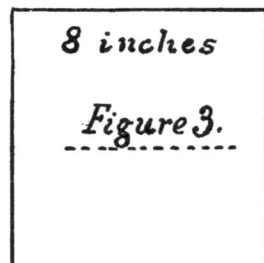

```
Figure 1.

16 inches
Square
```

```
                                    8 inches
Figure 2.              Figure 3.
16 inches
```

(8 inches — left side of Figure 2)

The first thing is to learn to cut the pattern, as Figure 1. Fold it across the middle as Figure 2. Fold it once

48

more, making it a square again, as Figure 3. Now do the
rest of the folding from the center at *a.* Fold diagonally
across from *a* to *b*, as Figure 4. Then fold *a—c* to *a—b*,
measure the line *a—c*, and mark the same length from *a*,
along the line toward *d*, as Figure 5. Draw a line from
d to *c*, that shall be at all points equally distant from *a*,
which means it will be very slightly curved as Figure 6.
Cut along this line from *d* to *c* and open it out, and you
will have the round disk, Figure 7, which makes the pattern
for the buckram brim of a Gainsborough hat.

The headsize in pressed hats and bought frames is
sometimes round, and as few human heads are of that
form, we have many hats that press on the forehead, and
leave gaps on the side, and never feel comfortable, nor stay
on well. This is all unnecessary. Take a piece of stiff
paper, or better still, of cardboard, and cut out a headsize
that perfectly fits the head. Make it a little larger than

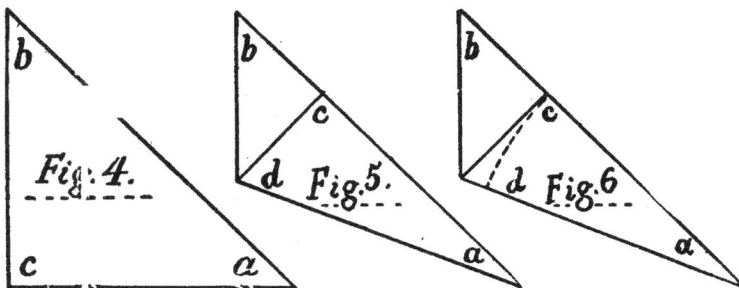

the perfect fit, to allow for a thickness of velvet, which must
come into the headsize from this under side of the brim,
and also for the lining. By placing two fingers within the
headsize, the measure will be perfect when finished. Lay
the headsize pattern on the brim disk, so that the center of

the headsize will be exactly over the center of the brim disk. Mark around it and cut it out to the line.

Now lay the pattern of the brim on a piece of milliner's buckram. Cut around the outer edge. Mark around the headsize and lift the pattern. Cut out the headsize, leaving an inch of the buckram all the way round within the headsize mark. This is to slit and turn up in the crown, as in

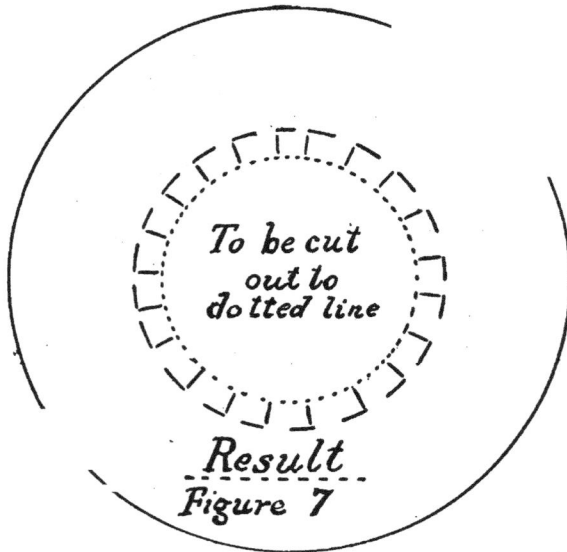

To be cut out to dotted line

Result

Figure 7

Figure 7. The smooth side of the buckram is always the upper side of the brim and the outside of the crown.

Fashion changes the outlines of the brim, making it longer from front to back and from side to side, but the round brim is the standard one. Likewise. the headsize is sometimes placed nearer the front and again it may be nearer the back, but the center is the conservative place for it.

Take brace wire, the kind frames are made of, and sew it around the edge of the brim, placing it on the upper side of the buckram just so it will not show from the upper side.

Overcast it, as Figure 8, using No. 5 millinery needles and No. 24 D millinery thread. Any needle and any thread would do, but the milliner's thread, which is heavily waxed and made of great strength so each stitch will tell, is far preferable to any other thread, and the milliner's needle has the long reach that no other needle has.

Figure 8—The Gainsborough crown

The wiring should begin in the back and when around, overlap the wire two inches and keep it flat by overcasting one stitch and the next stitch, placing between the wires. Never let one wire get on top of another, for it would make a bulge in the fabric, with which you cover the frame.

If the brim is as large as the 16-inch Gainsborough, double wiring of the edge will be necessary. Put on the second wire within the first one, overcasting one stitch, over the brim edge, and the next stitch inserting between the wires. The ends have two inches overlay, and are stitched down flat as the first one is, and as close to it as possible.

Next wire the headsize, around the marked line, on the right side of the buckram.

Begin in the back and overlay the wire two inches, stitching it down flat. One more brace wire is needed be-

51

tween the headsize and the brim edge. It is put on with the usual overlap, and secured by a stitch from the under side of the buckram, which merely goes through on one side of the wire, and directly across and down on the other side, the long stitch being on the under side. This is done in order to leave as little thread on the right side as possible. The brim is now finished.

The regular Gainsborough crown is high and straight on the sides, and flat on top. Fashion greatly modifies it now, and the soft crowned variety seems to be liked the best. If it is desired to have it conform enough to go around the headsize, which is probably longer than it is wide, take a piece of straight buckram 2¾ inches wide, and

Figure 9—The Gainsborough Brim, wired

long enough to go around the headsize, outside of the wire, allow quarter of an inch space between the wire and crown, for the velvet covering of the crown will be turned in there. Overlap the buckram an inch and stitch down smoothly.

Wire both top and bottom overcasting, so the wire can not be seen from the right side. Allow the usual overlap of wire, which secure so it will lie perfectly flat. Take the headsize you cut in the pasteboard and lay it on a piece of paper and mark around it. Cut the paper thus marked, allowing one inch outside of the marked line. This will give a pattern for the crown top. Make it out of crinoline, and lay it in small plaits around the edge, about two inches apart, and all folded in the same direction. These plaits should be of the same depth and made so that they will take up enough of the fulness so that this crown top will just fit into the upper wire of the side crown. Stitch down the plaits smoothly and tack the crown top inside of the upper wire of the side crown (see Figure 9) and the frame is completed.

DUCHESS OF
DEVONSHIRE

The World Famed Portrait
by
Thos. Gainsborough
which is responsible for
fixing the artist's name on
this character of hat

LESSON X

Varying the Buckram Frame

We will now consider the varying of the flat buckram frame, and show first what can be done with the round Gainsborough brim.

Suppose we should wish a drooping shape. The brim in that case would be slashed from the brim edge to the headsize, leaving just enough cloth to hold it together at the headsize. Then overlap these slashed sections at the

No. 1. Slashing and overlapping the brim.　　No. 2. The drooping brim, ready to be turned

brim edge, and all in the same direction, as shown in Fig. 1. Stitch them around the brim edge, and the shape will be more or less drooping, according to the amount of overlap. It will be found that a very little overlap will make quite a drooping brim, and it is better to slash the brim in many places and overlap but slightly, rather than to cut in few places and make the overlap large.

In doing the latter, the brim edge will be scalloped and

54

irregular. Should the droop desired be very slight indeed, the brim can be slashed in only a few cuts, say four, but the overlap must be small, and if a greater droop is wanted, it should be obtained by more slashes rather than greater overlaps.

If the drooping brim is made of an old straight one this method is necessarily used, after all the wires are removed, except the headsize wire. But if the drooping brim is to be cut from new buckram, make a pattern first, like the Gainsborough brim, and slash and overlap the pattern until the desired droop is attained, then cut one slash clear through the headsize line, and lay the pattern out flat, as in Figure 2, and lay it on the buckram, and cut the brim in one continuous piece, allowing one inch extra on either edge, where the last slash was made, for an overlap, to join the brim together, at the back.

As by overlapping, and so contracting the brim edge,

No. 3. Making a portrait brim by expanding it   No. 4. Transforming a hat into a turban brim

we can make the drooping brims, so by putting in gores or gussets, and thus expanding the brim edge, we can make rolling or turned up shapes, as in Figure 3. This one inset will serve to make a hat turn up in the back, or roll on the side, and give all sorts of delightful curves to the rest of the brim.

Changing a Hat Into a Turban

Figure 4 shows how the brim may be slashed, and turned up, and overlapped, to change it into a turban, and also explains how the brim edge can be given little slashes of the same depth and overlapped to make a standing edge.

Figure 5 shows a ripple brim made by the inset of many gores at regular intervals. By experimenting with overlaps and gussets, all sorts of results may be produced. They

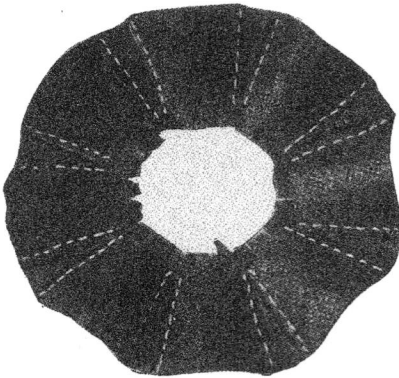

No. 5. Gussets produce a ripple effect   No. 6 Sloping the crown by means of plaits

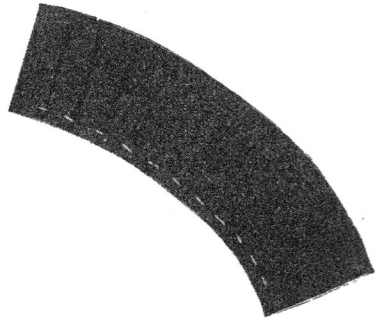

should first be cut in stiff paper patterns and sewed to shape and fitted to the head before cutting from the buckram.

Generally the fancy buckram shapes are purchased from the manufacturers, but it is very essential that every milliner should know how to produce varied shapes from the plain piece of buckam, as there may be places and times when she could not procue them in the usual way, when badly needed, and for the home economist it is always well to know how to change last year's shape into this year's.

Removing Dents in a Used Shape

If the shape has been used, and dents are in it, they can commonly be removed by holding the shape over the tea kettle spout for a few moments and pressing it into the proper form with the fingers. If this process is not sufficient for the brim, wipe a slightly dampened cloth over it, and press with a very moderate iron and with a piece of tissue paper or thin cloth between the buckram and the iron. If the buckram is made too damp or the iron is too hot it will stick.

If there are overlaps or gores in the frame and it is to be covered with velvet in smooth plain form, one thickness of flannelette or thin sheet wadding, laid on the upper side of the brim will hide all irregularities. It should be cut so it will be perfectly smooth and not overlap in any place.

In making a soft crown or a stiff one, the side crown is often sloped, sometimes contracting as it goes toward the crown top and sometimes flaring out. These results can be accomplished by slashing the plain straight side crown as in Figure 6, and then the broader edge can be placed next to the headsize, if a contrasting side crown is desired, or the narrower edge can be used next to the headside, and the side crown will then flare at the crown top. If it is desired to cut the side crown in one piece, fit a straight pattern, that is slashed and overlapped as Figure 6, on the buckram and cut it in one continuous piece, allowing one inch on either end for the overlap in closing it, at the back.

The brim edge itself can be changed in shape anywhere and to any amount. It can be shortened in the back by cutting away a long sloping portion, or in the same manner the front can be shortened, on either or both sides. The brim edge will have to be cut down if a turban or toque is made out of a plain Gainsborough brim, otherwise it would stand up too high. Take a plain Gainsborough brim, shorten it to half its width in the back and let it gradually widen to the brim edge in front, then slash the back from the brim edge to the headsize, and overlap at the brim edge until it almost droops into the neck. Next slash directly in front from the brim edge to the headsize, overlap at the brim edge, and a poke brim will be produced. It may need more or less overlapping in the front or back to fit any certain face, and the brim edge can be changed slightly to make it more becoming.

Remember, lastly, that there is no limit to the possibilities of a plain piece of buckram with gussets and overlaps.

Typical Hat of Rococo Period (1770)

LESSON XI

Emergencies in Frame Making

Before leaving the subject of frame work, we will have a few suggestions for emergencies. Suppose you suddenly need a round crown and none are at hand or procurable. If you have a mold or form, and buckram, one can be made nicely by setting overnight. The mold is commonly made of plaster of Paris, held together with hair fibres of some sort. However, there are workers in fine hard woods, who supply many forms for milliner's use.

A piece of buckram that will extend an inch beyond the mold, clear around, is cut from the roll. The pattern can be obtained by measuring the mold fom the headsize to the center at the top of the crown, and over the opposite side to the headsize again. This will give the diameter of a circle, which can be cut from paper, allowing the extra inch around its edge. Place this pattern on the buckram and cut it out. Pass the buckram rapidly under a faucet, shaking off every drop of water that will come, then place it on the mold, with the center of the buckram over the center of the top of the mold.

To Make Buckram Pliable

A very little water makes buckram pliable so it can be easily stretched. In fact, after a few moments standing it seems to get wetter and wetter all the time. So be sure it has not too much moisture to begin with. Draw down the buckram across the straight of the goods and again across the straight of the goods at right angles, dividing the buckram into four equal parts. The straight of the buckram will not stretch very much, but the bias will. Pull down the bias at the bottom and work it down from the top, and the opposite (bias) side treat in the same way. Then take the bias sides at right angles and pull them down in like manner. Nearly all the creases can be worked out, with patience, and when finally it is as smooth as possible, take a good stout string and tie it very tight, about an inch above the bottom of the mold. This string can be turned over and over as you work it downward, all the while getting tighter and tighter. Stop at the bottom, where the string will stay, when the crown is taken off of the mold, and will mark the place to trim off the buckram, and then sew on the wire around the headsize.

If this crown is made in the evening and allowed to set until the next morning it will be almost dry, and in the proper state to take off the form.

It may stick a little, but by careful work can be removed without spoiling the shape. It must dry perfectly before it is trimmed off about the headsize, and the wire sewed on, when it is complete.

Suppose you were in the country, away from all marts of trade, and had no buckram. Take crinoline, and if it were the stiff kind, one thickness is first taken, exactly as the buckram was dampened and then put over the form. Go over it with a brush and shellac, weak glue, or flour paste, if nothing better offers. Put on a second layer of the crinoline, exactly as the first, only the last layer is not treated to the shellac or glue. Work out all the wrinkles possible and tie the string, as in the buckram. Be sure the shellac, glue or paste is put on lightly, not making the crinoline too wet, or it will adhere to the mold. If no mold is available, it is astonishing what forms one can get from common household utensils. One can make a pretty crown, stretched over the bottom of a serving dish. There are always bowls, cans, pitchers or pans, that can give shape to a crown. If the utensil proves too shallow, make the upper portion of the crown and piece it down with paper, getting the proper slope, and use the paper as a pattern to cut out buckram or whatever stiffening material is at hand and sew it on the bottom of the crown.

The crown made of crinoline should be treated just as the buckram in its finishing. When the crinoline is soft and rather flimsy it takes three thicknesses to make a good crown. Put the sizing or stiffening over the first and second layers, but not over the outside one. Colorless shellac can be bought at the drug store and dissolved in alcohol and kept in a bottle for instant use, or a regular white shellac can be purchased already prepared. In the wholesale millinery houses, a milliner's shellac absolutely colorless will be found on sale. It can be used for many things besides frames. Two ribbons may be shellacked together to give two-toned effects. It is also used to lacquer leaves and quills.

If a special shape is desired and there is no mold to form it, make a crown or brim of very strong wire, placing the stay wires not more than an inch apart, and let the tie wires be twisted together on the opposite side from where the buckram will be used. The tie wire would necessarily make a little hump in the buckram, which is to be avoided. Use this crown or brim just as you would a mold, and it will be found useful.

Willow mesh is also used for crowns, and when dipped in sizing can be stretched into almost any shape. It must be carefully handled as it ravels easily. It is liked for collapsible crowns.

Copying a Buckram Frame

Suppose a copy of a buckram frame must be had at once, with no chance of molding overnight. Take the crown first. The mold, wire frame or buckram crown itself, which is to furnish the pattern, is laid over with soft brown paper, pressed down carefully from the top toward the base, working the fulness into as few creases as possible. When the paper gives a perfect imitation of the shape of the mold, wire frame, or buckram crown, mark all the creases with a lead pencil, both where the fold is laid back on itself and where it meets the goods under it. Remove the paper, straighten it out, and cut out all the superfluous paper contained in the creases. Lay this pattern on the buckram, allow a quarter of an inch margin beyond all the penciled lines for overlapping. Bring these overlaps of the creases together so that the penciled lines will be exactly over each other, and stitch in place. Get the distance from the top of the crown to the headsize all around and cut off the buckram at the headsize and wire it. There may be little projections or fulness where the creases begin in the buckram. Dampen the finger very slightly, place some hard round object underneath and press down firmly from the right side and the projection will disappear.

You will find this quickly made frame a perfect copy. The brim has been spoken of at length in former lessons, but to recapitulate, the flat brim can be always draughted directly on the buckram and cut from it. It can be given the various shapes by overlaps and gussets. It can also be molded on the convex side of a wire brim, used as a mold. The buckram in that case is dampened and stitched or pinned down around the edge.

If you wish to give a curve to a straight buckram brim, slash the buckram across its grain and bias to the curve you wish to make. Make two slashes about 2 inches apart.

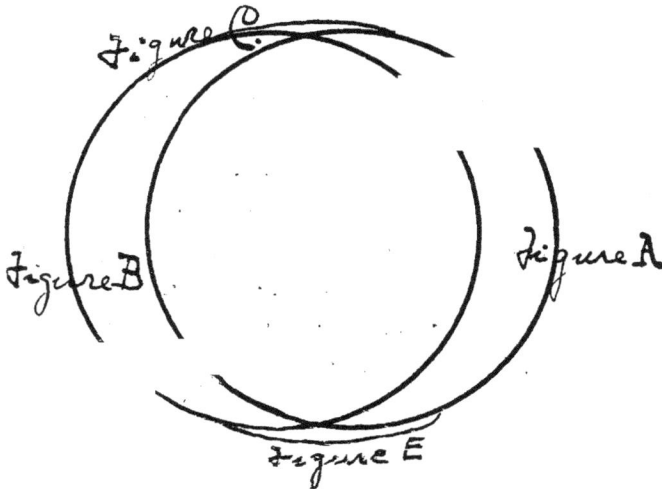

Take a moderately hot iron and pass over the buckram, lifting up one edge of the iron and curving it in the direction desired. For instance, if the side brim is to be curved, slash it twice on the bias, then place the iron on its edge at the headsize and move toward the brim edge, giving the iron a rounding movement. Experiments with making curves with an iron, cutting patterns and molding crowns will lead to wonderful results if persisted in.

Before we leave this subject we will suggest a substitute for a bandeau. Take a piece of crinoline, roll it into a tube one and a half inches in diameter, stitch it so it will not unroll but so the hollow tube is preserved. Place it at the headsize within the hat lining and secure it with a few tie stitches. It will be pliable and will adjust itself to any head.

Tissue paper can be used in the same way, but is not so satisfactory, as it packs in time and is rather heating.

To make an oblong pattern for a flat buckram brim, cut the round disk, as shown in the former lesson. Take a larger piece of paper, place the disk upon it, and draw a line around its edge (see Figure A). Determine how much longer the final pattern is to be, and mark the distance from the brim edge at Figure B. Slip the disk over to Figure B and draw a second circle around its edge. Place the flat of the forearm opposite the center of the two circles, and putting a pencil on the brim edge at C, with a free hand movement, holding the flat of the arm as an axis, make the dotted line D. Turn the pattern, and make a similar line E. This cut out will give the elongated sides, or a brim longer front and back, according to how the crown is placed. The extra width is determined by how far over the second outline of the disk is drawn from the first.

LESSON XII

Covering the Buckram Frame

After considering the construction of the buckram frame and its variations we will next take up the covering of it. The brim edge of a buckram frame is sharp and cutting and must be padded before the velvet is put on. Any velvet too badly damaged for exterior use may be cut into bias strips, half an inch wide, and commencing at the back, placed evenly over the edge, swinging back and forth, with stitches about one-third of an inch on either side. When bringing the ends together do not overlap them, but bring

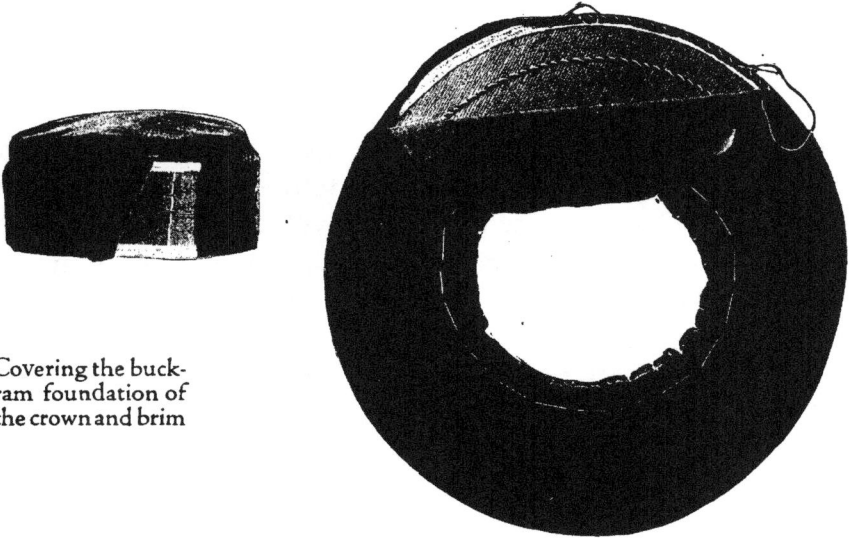

Covering the buck-
ram foundation of
the crown and brim

them together and cut off squarely, so they meet, and there will be no double thickness. This is called rough binding.

Old velvet, silk or cotton fabrics can be used, and preferably should be cut on the bias. The under brim may have a thickness of crinoline, flannelette or sheet wadding, laid over it, to keep the wires from showing through the velvet. It should be caught down by stitching it to the binding of the brim edge, after it has been carefully pinned in place. Cut it off even with the brim edge.

Applying the Fabric to the Brim

Now the brim is ready to cover with velvet. Place the bias of the velvet at the front of the upper side of the brim. Secure it to the brim edge with a pin, which we call the placing pin. Smooth out the velvet over the brim, so the goods will lie on the bias, from the front to the back. Put in a pin on the brim edge, where the straight of the velvet comes, next to the placing pin. Follow the straight of the goods to the opposite side, and pull it sufficiently to make the velvet very smooth. Put a pin in the brim edge to secure it. Next pin down the straight of the goods, at right angles, in the same manner. The four bias spaces between can now be pulled down until the velvet smooths out perfectly, then pin it in place. These pins should be all around the brim edge, about one inch apart, and all pointing toward the center of the brim. Cut off the velvet, so it projects half inch beyond the brim edge. Turn it over the brim edge and catch it down to the rough binding in short stitches, as shown in illustration.

Stitch around the headsize wire with stitches half an inch long on the right side and short ones on the under side. Let this stitching come just under the headsize wire from the direction of the brim edge, and to take up all fulness place the needle at an angle of forty-five degrees to the brim and come back from the other side at the same slant. This draws the velvet under the headsize wire and makes the stitching disappear.

Facing the Brim

Next put the velvet on the under side of the brim. Take a bias of the velvet, and pin it at the front of the brim, underneath. Smooth out the goods, pin it so the bias goes across the center of the underbrim, then pin the velvet on the straight of the goods next to the placing pin and stretch it across on the straight of the velvet to the other side. Then take the two straight places on the brim edge that are at right angles and secure them in the same way. All the remaining fulness can be taken up as the four bias places are drawn down and secured. Cut off the velvet, leaving a projection of half inch beyond the brim edge. Turn this in even with the upper edge and blind-stitch it to the velvet of the upper brim, on the very brim edge. The stitches should be even and about a quarter inch long. Watch that the thread as it comes from the upper into the lower velvet edge is so arranged as to come straight across, in which case it entirely disappears as the two edges are drawn together. For if the thread is slanting it will show. Baste around the headsize, about an inch outside of the headsize wire, and use a fine needle, as it has to go through the velvet on the upper side of the brim, and as small punctures as possible are desirable. Use the fine thread, because it has to be removed and leaves less markings.

Cut out the headsize of the under and upper velvet, leaving an inch to turn up into the crown and baste it into the headsize above the wire with long stitches on the inside next to the head. If it should bind, slash it, as the buckram was slashed. Straighten the slashed buckram in the head-size so that it will stand up withiñ the crown. Take the two thicknesses of velvet with it, and overcast them together around the upper edge, keeping the upright position.

The crown is next to cover. Rip out the top crown, take out the small plaits and smooth it out with the hand or press it with a very moderate iron. The markings of the plaits must not be obliterated. Baste this lining of the top crown to the wrong side of the velvet, with the bias at the front, and cut it out. Lay over the plaits as marked on the lining, and baste them down again. Cut a bias piece of the velvet as wide as the side crown, with an added inch on either edge, and long enough to go around the side crown. A little of the width will be taken up by stretching the velvet around in place, and the extra width that is left will be lapped over the top and bottom edge, making the lapovers even.

Start in the back, cut the bias velvet across from top to bottom of the side crown, turn in half inch, and pin it down. Stretch the velvet from this point around the side crown, drawing it tight enough to lay nice and smooth, and bring the end to the place of starting. Cut it off square, turn in half inch and blind-stitch it to the piece that is laid under at the beginning. The lapovers may be laced back and forth from the upper edge to the lower edge on the inside with the saddler's stitch, which will be found in the lesson on "Stitches."

The rough binding of the side crown is a matter of dispute among milliners. Some use no binding at all, some bind the upper edge and some bind both edges. If the rough binding is used, the overlaps on the side crown can be secured to the binding with the same stitch that is shown in sewing the upper velvet of the brim to the rough binding. In any case, 'the stitching on the side crown velvet must not be seen from the right side.

Now tack in the top crown, and this can be done with a long stitch on the inside and a short one brought through barely over the top of the side crown, but toward the crown top, and enough on the inside so it does not show from the outside. With the long millinery needle this can be accomplished and draw it up tight with the stout thread and all stitching will disappear.

Place the crown on the center of the brim. Take a stitch under the side crown where it lies on the brim, and then thrust the needle through the brim with a stilting stitch. Pull the thread firmly to the right, on the under side of the brim, and it will make a tiny opening in the fabric, where the needle first came through. While the thread is held very taut, insert the point of the needle into the tiny hole at the thread base, incline the needle at right angles from which it came through the brim, in the first place, and the thread will be drawn back through the hole and entirely disappear if no portion of the fabric has been allowed to come between the thread base and the needle point. This is called the "Hidden Stitch." (See lesson on "Stitches.") If the threads of the goods are slightly disarranged by pulling the thread they can easily be put in place with the needle point. This stitching is continued around the crown, and finally secured within the headsize.

A crown is put on with a tie stitch, when a fold is to be placed at the crown base to hide the stitches, but even then the hidden stitch should be used on the under side of the brim.

In a few exceptional cases the crown is sewed on before the under side of the brim is covered. Some silks and other closely woven materials show every prick of the needle, and then we sew on the crown first and cover the under side of the brim afterwards. It is an awkward job at best and is rarely necessary.

In many of the bought frames there is an upward projection of the brim, around the headsize, that makes it possible to sew the crown to the headsize without leaving stitches that will show after the lining is sewed in. If the material on the underside of the brim is left loose at the headsize and the crown is small enough to fit close to the headsize of the brim the fabric from the under brim may be held back sufficiently to sew the crown to the brim headsize, and afterwards the fabric from the under brim may be carefully smoothed into the headsize and stitched to the slashed buckram that stands upright within the headsize.

Lastly, the lining is put in as shown in a former lesson and the Gainsborough hat is complete.

Mid-Victorian Styles 1860 70

LESSON XIII

Brim Finishes

Most of the variations of a brim covering are introduced by covered wires. The illustration shows three sections of the brim, each exemplifying a different method of

No. 1   No. 2

No. 3

brim covering. In No. 1 heavy cable wire is sewed to the upper side of the brim on its brim edge, but not over it, for the circumference does not want to be increased. When the ends of the wire come together, after going around the brim edge, do not overlap them, but let them touch, making a complete circle.

Cable wire is the largest millinery wire used, and is covered with a cotton filling, and then wound around with silk thread. It will usually allow a needle to go through the filling, and the wire should be caught on its underside and tacked to the brim edge, for an overcast stitch, unless it went in very closely under the wire, would prevent later the proper use of the velvet covering.

Next put on the velvet or fabric of the upper brim, as instructed in former lesson. Take strong thread, preferably of the same color as the velvet, and stitch the velvet down close under the cable wire, on the side toward the headsize. Take stitches one-quarter of an inch long on the right side, and incline the needle outward, toward the brim edge, at an angle of 45 degrees, and go through the buckram and make a short stitch on the under side. When the thread is drawn tight it will disappear under the cable wire. After this is completed, take the velvet over the cable wire, down under the brim edge, and fasten it to the rough binding of the frame, as formerly shown. Be sure that the velvet or fabric is perfectly smooth over the wire, without a wrinkle. The wire will now stand on the brim edge, making a clearly defined finish.

The underbrim velvet is now brought up, turned in, and blindstitched to the upper side, the stitching coming through, on the upper side, at the crease under the cable wire.

The cut shows a cable wire inserted between the upper and lower covering of the brim. This cable wire is covered separately with a bias piece of velvet, and is then sewed to the velvet from the upper side of the brim, where it is brought over the brim edge, and secured to the rough binding. The wire projects slightly beyond the brim edge, and is fastened to the velvet, with the same stitch used in securing the velvet to the rough binding.

Lastly, the velvet from the upper brim is brought up and turned in against the wire; and the upper brim velvet and the lower brim velvet are blindstitched together, going through the velvet that covers the cable wire, and letting the wire project beyond the blindstitching. This makes a plain, substantial and well made brim edge.

Inserting the Brim Wire

No. 3 shows where the raised and covered cable wire is set far in from the brim edge. The upper side of the brim is first covered with the velvet, from the headsize to where the raised wire is wanted. This should be marked off beforehand with a pencil, describing a circle at a regular distance from the brim edge. Allow one-quarter of an inch extra for the wire to rest upon. It should be carefully basted down around this edge, far enough in so there will be no danger of its fraying. Cut out a circle of paper, having the diameter of the brim, as you were taught in a former lesson on the Gainsborough hat. Cut out the center of this pattern, while it is folded, so that it will leave a circle extending from the brim edge, and overlapping the velvet from the headsize by one inch. Lay the pattern on the velvet and cut it out, allowing one-quarter of an inch on its outer edge to come over the brim edge and be secured to the rough binding on the frame. Place this circle of velvet on the brim and baste it down one-half inch from the brim edge. Put the cable wire under the inner edge of this circle of velvet, pass the velvet over it, and tuck the edge well under the wire. This edge sometimes has to be clipped with little gashes, that it may stretch sufficiently to lie smoothly. Now stitch down the velvet under the wire, inclining the needle at an angle of forty-five degrees toward the headsize, and making the stitching from the side of the wire nearest the brim edge. The stitches should be one-quarter of an inch long, with the short stitch on the under side. When the thread is tightly drawn it will disappear. This gives a truly stylish finish to a brim, and as many wires can be introduced as desired, one fitted circle of velvet being overlaid by another.

If the distance between the wires is small, a bias piece of velvet could be used instead of the circle. The bias piece should be stretched on the outer edge, and held in as small space as possible on the wire, yet it must be smooth. The bias piece, used in this way, always necessitates a seam in the back, which must be made by turning in each end and blindstitching them together. This does not leave so nice a finish as the smooth circle. The cable wires may be placed anywhere, from between the upper and lower brim coverings to the headsize. Great ingeniousness may be displayed in their arrangement.

LESSON XIV

Covering the Crown

To cover the crown with any fabric requires the same treatment for a flat top crown, the bowl shape, or the rounding elongated one.

The straight of the goods is brought down in front and folded under the headsize wire and pinned in place, then the fabric is carried up and over the center of the top crown to the back, all the while on the straight of the goods. Turn it under the headsize and pin down as in front.

Pinning the Fabric to Place

Next, the two straight places in the goods at right angles to the front and back are drawn down on the sides

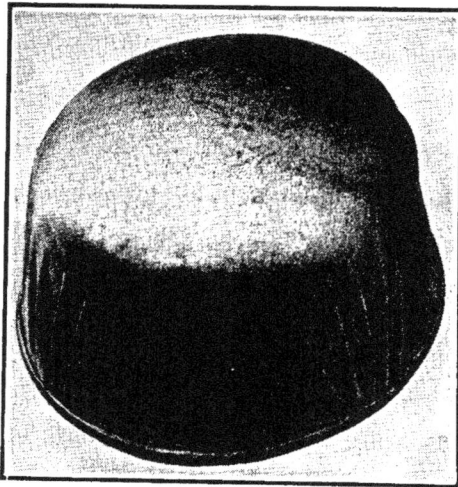

The stiffened crown, ready to join to brim.

and turned under the headsize wire and pinned in place so that it will divide the space around the headsize into four equal parts and also equally dispose of the fulness of the goods. A few inches on either side of the direct front the fabric can be drawn down and pinned under the headsize without leaving any crease near the crown top. This space depends upon the pliability of the cloth. The more pliable, the larger the space that will lie smoothly at the front and over the crown top to the back pinning. The same is true of the sides, and if the crown is oval, the plain spaces on the sides will be larger than the front and back. Pin all these four smooth places down firmly and you will find all the fulness is confined to small spaces, four in number. These are all on the bias. Pull the goods down firmly to the headsize. Each space is now covered by five small plaits of the goods and are laid in the same direction in each of the four spaces. These plaits are laid so that they touch at the bottom and spread out toward the crown top like the ribs of a fan. You will find by experiment that any direction can be given to these plaits in proportion as you pull the fabric on the upper or lower side of the plait. To lay them exactly takes patience and care, but can be readily done with practice.

The headsize may be finished with a binding, as in the illustration, or overcast and the stitching hidden later with a finishing fold or the milliner's fold, and often the headsize is completed by simply turning under the goods and sewing it around with the stilting stitch, without any other finish.

The soft crown was explained in the covering of the Gainsborough hat. A heavy wire covered with the goods adds much to the appearance of a soft crown, when it is introduced at the top of the side crown. That can be done in the same manner in which it is used on the brim edge. That is, it may be inserted under the fabric of the side crown itself and stitched down to make the edge finish at the top of the side crown, or the wire may be covered separately and sewed in between the side crown and the crown top. Sometimes a heavy wire is also placed as a finish at the headsize. It can be introduced in either of the ways described relative to the wire at the top of the side crown.

The Two-Piece Crown Covering

Another method of covering the crown is that in which two pieces of velvet or other fabric are used, one to cover the crown top, and another, cut on the bias, for the side crown. Take a round crown or an oval one, as shown in the illustration, mark off a line 3 inches above the headsize wire, completely around the crown. This will define the base of the crown top. Place a bias of the goods at the front and on this line and pin it there. This is the placing pin. Next take the straight of the fabric, on the right front, let it run across the crown top to the left back, on the straight, and secure both places with pins on the line drawn for the base of the crown top. Draw down the goods at right angles and pin on the line. Now you will find that the four remaining spaces can be drawn down to the line at the base of the crown top until all creases will disappear and the crown top will be perfectly smooth. Pin it down at the line carefully and stitch it around with a stitch one-quarter of an inch on the outside and very small on the inside.

Stretching the Goods to Assure Smoothness

Cut a bias strip of goods long enough to go entirely around the side crown and, to turn in half an inch on either end where it comes together. This piece must be broad · enough to turn one-third inch on both the upper and lower edge. To make it perfectly smooth it will have to be stretched around the side crown, and as this always lessens the width, it is best to stretch it around before cutting to get some estimate of its width. If the side crown slants outward as it goes toward the headsize, stretch the goods most on its lower edge so it will fit the side crown. Commence in the back and turn in the end of the bias piece half an inch, then turn in the upper edge one-third of an inch and pin it around the crown top at the drawn line, so it will nicely cover the stitching that holds the crown top. This bias side crown must be fitted as you go, stretching the lower edge if it flares or so disposing the fabric that it will cover smoothly any irregularities. When it is around, turn in the end for half an inch, make the last turn in at the top, and bring the two ends together and blindstitch them down from the base of the crown top to the headsize. The upper edge of the side crown may be blindstitched to the crown top, or a few stitches may be used to hold it in place and keep it from slipping down.

Turn under the lower edge, inside of the crown, and overcast it about the crown base, if it is to be finished later with a fold about the crown base which will hide the stitching; and if not, sew it down with the tiniest stitch possible on the right side, just above the crown base wire and a stitch about one-quarter of an inch long on the inside of the crown. A wire of any size may be inserted under the upper edge of this bias side covering and sewed down in the manner before described. These things are matters of taste.

LESSON XV

Folds and Hems

Before leaving the velvet work we will consider several lines of embellishment where the velvet is used for decorative purposes.

First, we will take the folds. The finishing fold, designated by Figure 1 in the illustration, is a narrow bias piece of velvet, with the edges turned over on to the wrong side,

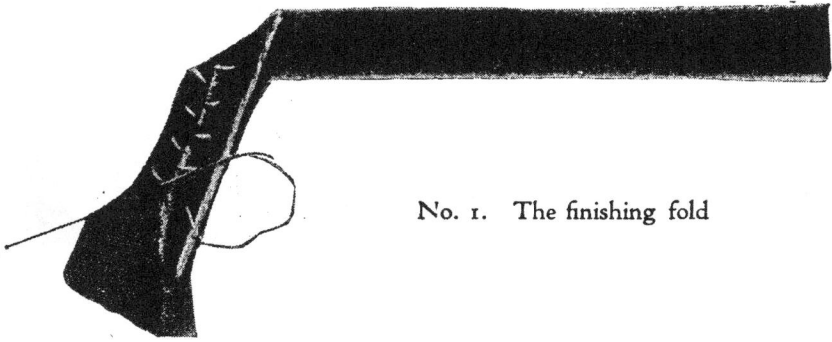

No. 1. The finishing fold

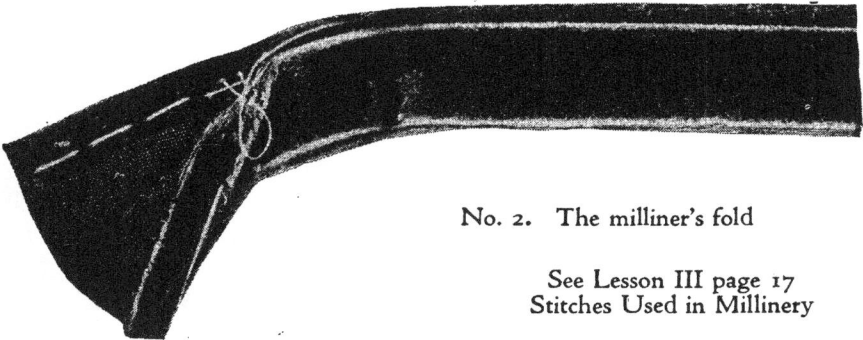

No. 2. The milliner's fold

See Lesson III page 17
Stitches Used in Millinery

and held together with the saddler's stitch (see lesson **on** Stitches). This finishing fold is used at the base of the crown to hide the sewing, when the crown is put on with visible stitches. It is drawn around the crown base, tight enough to decrease the width of the fold, but not so much as to detract from its beauty. Turn in the ends at the back and blind-stitch them together. If there is to be an ornament or bow placed anywhere about the crown, let the finishing fold end under the ornamentation. In such event the ends do not need to be turned in, but cut them off smoothly, where they come together, and sew them down firmly with visible stitches.

This fold is sometimes placed at the top of the side crown as a finish, or by slightly stretching one edge of the fold, it may be laid around the brim near its edge, or any-

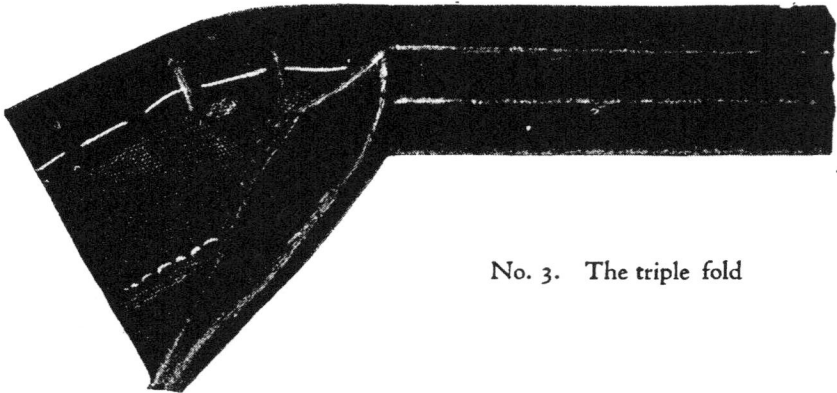

No. 3.   The triple fold

where from the brim edge to the headsize as taste may suggest. In using it in this manner it is blindstitched in position on its stretched edge only.

The Milliner's Fold, seen in Figure 2, is made of a wider piece of bias velvet than the finishing fold. The edge is turned over from the right side for the width of one-third of an inch and stitched in place on its lower edge with the long stitch on the side of the turned over edge, and the

80

short stitch on the right side of the velvet. Take the other edge of the velvet that has not been used, turn it over in the same manner as the first edge, and make it of the same width, but do not stitch it down until you bring it up on to the first edge which is folded over, then blindstitch the second edge to the first, leaving enough of the first to look like a cord above the second.

The milliner's fold can be used for the same purposes as the finishing fold, but when it is placed about a brim must be stretched on the plain edge, away from the corded effect, as there is too much sewing to admit of much elasticity.

These two folds are best adapted to velvet or silk, but can be used when made of any fabric provided it is not transparent.

The Triple Fold

The third illustration shows the triple fold. This takes a wider length of bias velvet than either of the two former folds. The edge is turned over and stitched down like the commencement of the two other folds and should be the same width. A small seam is now made in the velvet, paralled to the turned over edge, and on the wrong side of the goods. This seam must mark the termination of the opposite edge of the fold, and this edge must be of the same width as the first edge, and must also equal the width of the middle section of the completed fold. The middle section begins with the small seam (which must be held in direction toward the first turned over edge) and terminates with the turned in edge of the goods, which is blindstitched to the first turn over, leaving the three sections of equal width. Its construction can be seen in illustration.

Figure 4 shows the mourning folds, and they are particularly nice for crape or very soft goods of any kind. These

No. 4
Mourning folds

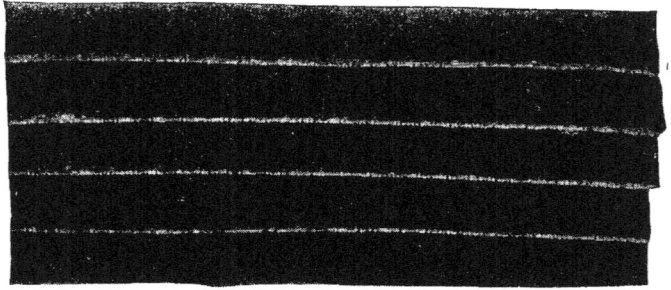

folds are sewed on some base, as buckram, rice net, crinoline, etc. The first fold is placed over the edge of this base, as a binding, and is stitched through and through, with equal stitches on either side. All the stitching on the mourning folds should be made as near the lower edge as will hold the goods firmly. The next fold is a bias piece, doubled, and sewed on by its lower edge, with the long stitch on the right side. The fold must be so placed that it will cover the sewing at the lower edge of the binding, and each succeeding fold must cover the stitching that holds the fold before it. The velvet of the last fold is made longer on one side than on the other, and this long side is taken over the edge of the base and tacked down on the wrong side of the base. The long side makes the outside of this last fold. The folds when completed should be of equal width. The name mourning fold is misleading, as they can be used equally well for hat bands, girdles, belts, or for dress trimming, and can be made of silk, satin, velvet, crepe or any fabric that will not show the stitching. They may be made in any number or width, and can be sewed directly on the side crown of a hat.

The Slip Stitch Hem

Next we will consider the various hems used in millinery. The first and most important is the slip-stitch hem designed to be used where no stitching is to be seen upon

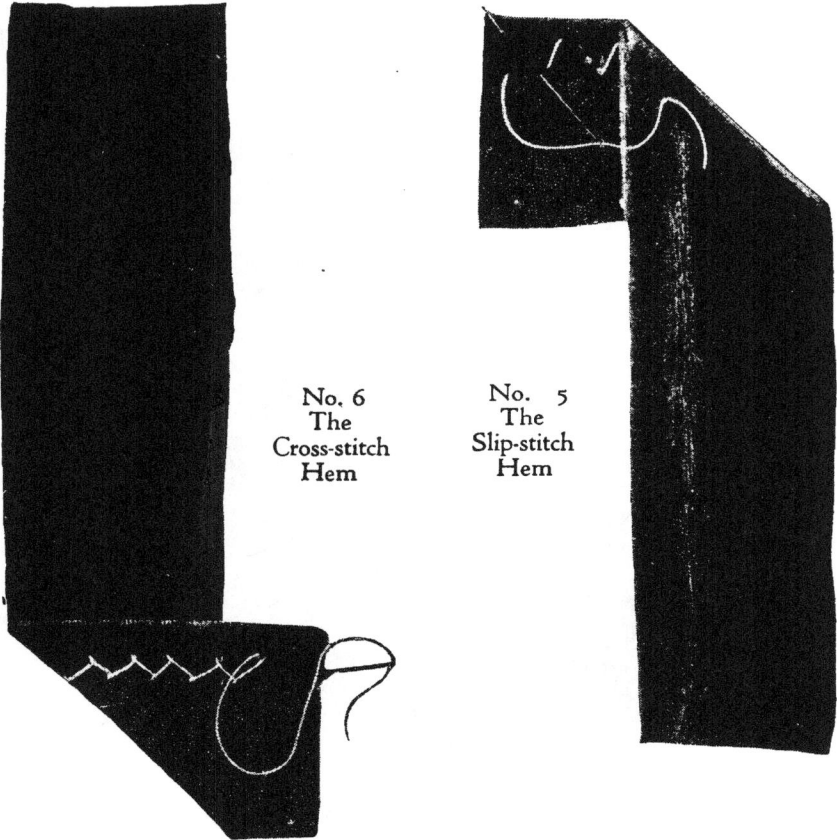

No. 6
The
Cross-stitch
Hem

No. 5
The
Slip-stitch
Hem

the right side, and only two folds of the goods employed. Take velvet, for instance, as in Figure 5, and turn over the edge on to the wrong side, for the width of one-third of an inch. Take up the fewest threads possible of the back weave of the velvet, never letting the needle go through the pile on the right side. Draw the thread through, and slip the needle under the turned over edge, nearly to its top, so that by no chance the raw edge could ravel out. Thrust the needle through, draw down the thread diagonally, and take another small stitch in the backing, and slip the needle under the turned over edge, as before. This gives a flat hem of only two thicknesses, and no visible stitches, and is

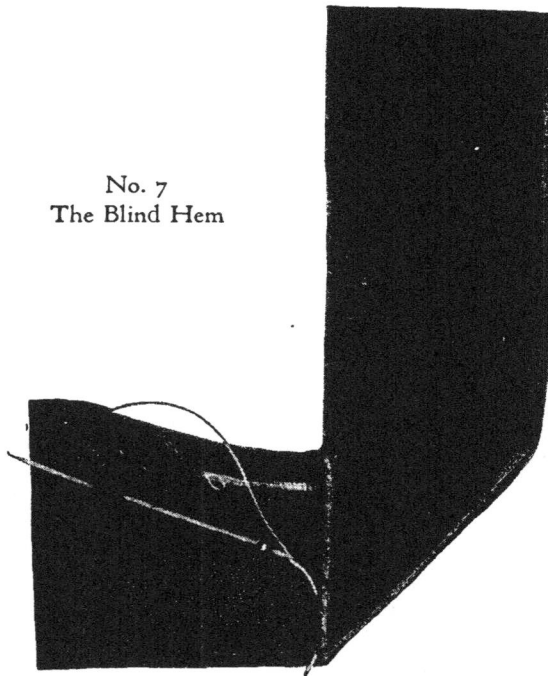

No. 7
The Blind Hem

very useful in millinery. It may be used in any goods, but stitches are most easily hidden in fabrics with a nap.

The Cross Stitch Hem

The cross stitch hem (Figure 6) is laid like the slip stitch hem, but is held in place by the cross stitch, sometimes called feather stitch (see lesson on Stitches) and the thread is never visible on the right side. The blind hem is made by turning over one-half inch of the goods on to the wrong side, and then tucking under the edge of the piece that is brought over from the right side as Figure 7. The needle is then inserted in the tube thus formed, and along its lower edge. Bring out the needle barely under this edge, pick up a few threads of the backing, exactly opposite the place where the needle comes through, insert again in the tube and continue this stitching, remembering all the time that stitches must be directly opposite so that when the thread is drawn taut all the stitching will disappear. Hence it is the blind hem.

The Cord Hem

The cord hem requires a wider piece of velvet than the former hems and is shown in Figure 8. A cord is covered

No. 8. The Cord Hem

with silk, or some other material, usually in colors. It is placed one and one-half inches from the edge of the goods, and basted down, with the cord itself farthest from the edge. The velvet is then drawn over the cording from the edge until it covers all but the narrow cord itself. Have it lie smoothly, holding the rough edge of the cord in a pocket-like fold of the velvet. Sew down the velvet so that the cord projects. This must be done with stitches sufficiently short to hold it firmly in place, as the velvet must be turned back again toward the edge and brought over and around the velvet pocket that holds the rough edge of the cording. Here it is slip-stitched, cross-stitched or blind-stitched down. This gives an edge of black velvet, for example, a cord of color, and both together make the cord hem. It is used when some color scheme is being carried out. Suppose the black velvet hat was trimmed with a pink, red or gold rose, and loops of black velvet were to complete the garniture. If they were finished with the cord hem, using the color to correspond with the rose, it would give a note of distinction. All these little schemes help to develop some dominant note in millinery, as beautiful and appropriate words transmit and embellish our thoughts.

Figure 3 shows a wider binding, and is called the half-stretched binding. One edge of this binding is slipstitched and the other is left raw, just as it was cut. The first thing to do is to measure this binding, to find where it must be stretched. The raw edge has to be sewed to the under side of the brim about one-third of an inch from the edge of both the binding and the brim edge. Measure the one-third of an inch that will extend from the raw edge of the binding to the place where the sewing will come. Then measure one-third of an inch back to the brim edge, as the slipstitched edge of the binding will be turned up and over the brim edge to the upper side of the brim. At the point where the velvet reaches the brim edge, hold it firmly by the forefinger and thumb of the right hand and place the forefinger of the left hand underneath and the thumb above, and pull and stretch the velvet toward the left, along the line where the brim edge will come, being very careful not to stretch either the slipstitched or the raw edge. Sew the raw edge on the under side of the brim edge, one-third of an inch from it; turn the binding over on the upper side, and it will lie smoothly, on account of the stretched brim edge.

The Full-Stretched Binding

Figure 4 shows the full stretched binding, the best one that is made. Both edges of this binding are slipstitched, and it is pulled and stretched, in the center of its width, as described in Figure 3. Cut the end of the binding square across, turn it in, and pin it at the back of the brim edge, with equal widths on the upper and lower sides. Stretch a little piece with the forefinger and thumb of the left hand, smooth it down with the right, and place another pin by sticking it clear though the brim and binding. Continue thus around the brim edge, turn in the last end of the binding and blindstitch the ends together. Sometimes the binding widens out at the ends. Place them at the correct wid·h on the upper side, rip a little of the slip-stitching on the under side and take up the extra width. It is only a matter of patience, for by this process it can be made perfect. If the binding has to be pieced, make the seam with the straight run of the goods, which will give a bias effect across the binding. Press the seam open carefully with the hands, as velvet will not stand an iron. It is best to place the piecing and the closing seam on the sides of the brim, as it is never desirable to have a piecing in front. The closing seam should be made on the bias, to correspond with the piecing seam. The closing is done with a blindstitch.

The full stretched binding is sometimes put on with wires. Then no slip-stitching is done on the edges of the binding, but they are left just as they are cut. The binding is stretched in middle of its length and pinned down about the brim edge, very tightly and smoothly drawn, and with the binding of equal width on both the upper and lower brim. It is basted down about one inch from the raw edges of the binding, a wire is slipped under the edge, the velvet tucked under the wire with a darning needle, and it is stitched in place with thread the color of the velvet, and if black it should not have a shiny finish. Never use silk, as it frays, breaks and works loose. The method of sewing down a wire is explained in a recent lesson. The needle is inclined at an angle of forty-five degrees under the wire, the stitch is made one-quarter of an inch long on the right side, and very small on the wrong side. When the thread is drawn up tightly it will entirely disappear under the wire. In putting on the full stretched binding with two wires sew on the under one first. The upper one is then sewed down, making the under stitch in such place as it will not show, hidden by the lower wire. Each stitch much be watched and made with care. The wired full stretched binding makes a very attractive edge for the brim.

The Extension Shirring for Broadening the Brim

To finish a brim edge, or more especially to make a brim larger, we have an extension shirring, shown in Figure 5. This consists of a bias piece of velvet, which may be simply gathered on the turned in edge, or a small tuck may be taken and a cord or wire be inserted when gathered or tucked and ready to be put on. It is sewed barely over the brim edge, on the upper and lower side, with the stilting stitch. It is very scant as to fulness, making merely an undulating line, instead of a ruffle.

This makes a narrow brim wide, and is often used to carry out a color scheme, being the color of flowers or feathers used to garnish the hat. If the extension shirring is very wide, it needs support. Lace wire bent into the form shown in Figure 6 and sewed around the upper brim, within the wiring of the brim edge, will support the brim extension, as this ruffled edge is slipped over the wire, one thickness above, and one below, and sewed on with a stilting stitch, so as to conceal the wire completely.

By putting on this extension shirring and giving a difrent curve to a brim edge, an old hat may be made to look decidedly new.

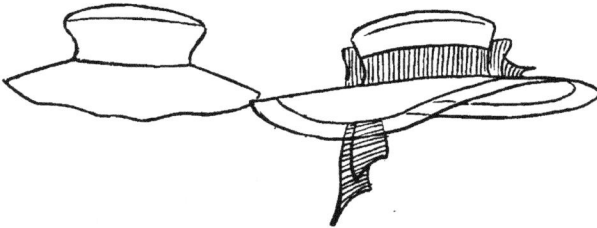

Before and After adding extension Brim

LESSON XVI

Brim Bindings

The first binding on a buckram frame is the rough binding, which serves a two-fold purpose. It pads the brim

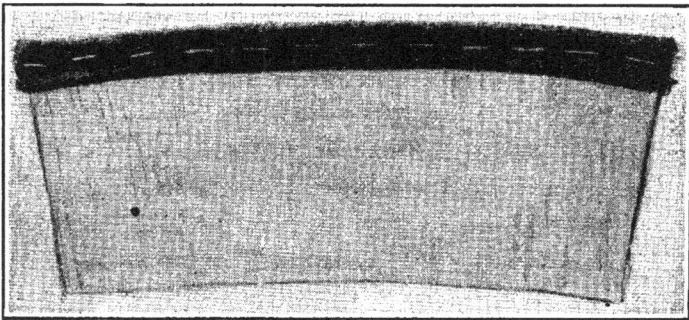

No. 1. Rough Binding

edge, and keeps the buckram from cutting the outside velvet, and it also acts as an anchor to the velvet of the upper

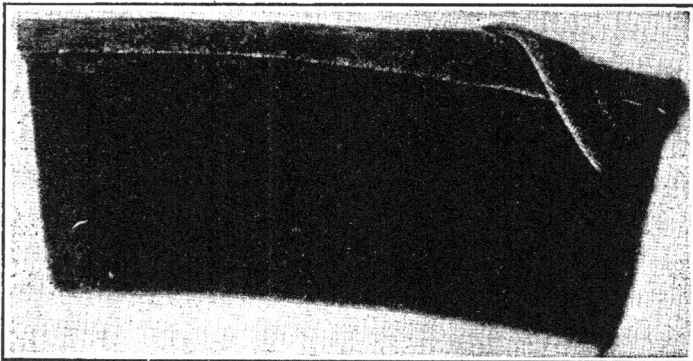

No. 2. Round Binding

brim, when it is brought over the brim edge and stitched down, as explained in a former lesson.

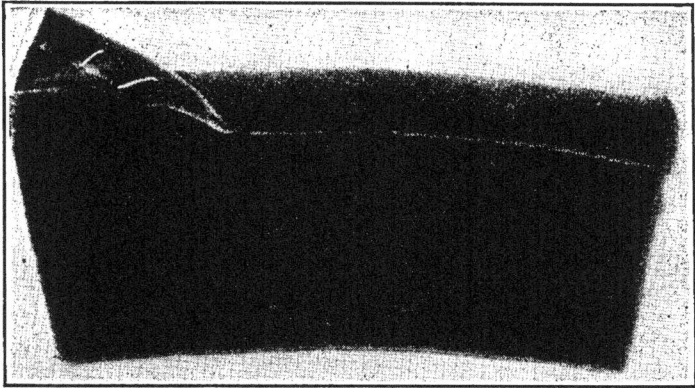

No. 3.   Half-stretched Binding

It is made of bias velvet, stretched smoothly and tightly around the brim edge, and sewed on with stitches one-quarter of an inch long, on either side.   Here is a good place

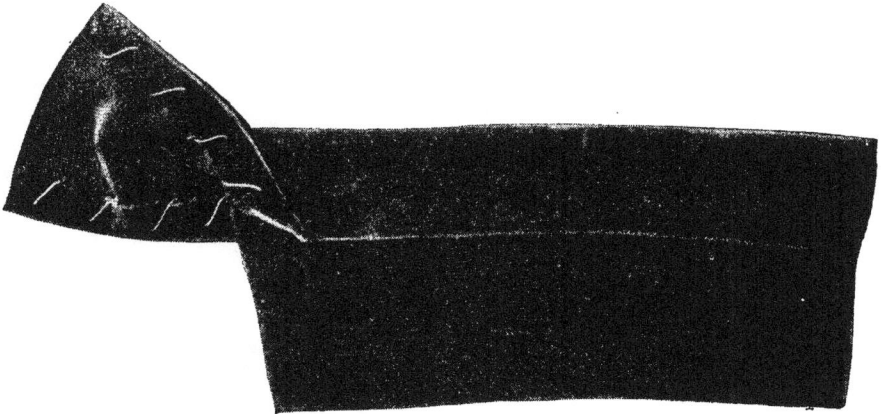

No. 4.   Full-stretched Binding

to dispose of old and discolored velvet, but there must be no overlapping when piecing is necessary, merely bring the ends together so they touch. Otherwise it would make a thick, knotty place on the brim edge.

The other three bindings are for the outside finish of the brim edge. When we use any one of these it is only

No. 5. Extension Shirring

necessary to bring the upper and lower velvet of the brim even with the brim edge. To do this, pin the upper velvet in place as described in a former lesson; baste it down with-

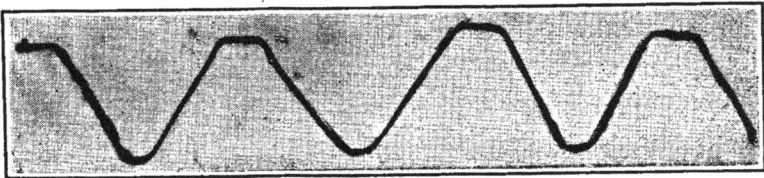

No. 6. Wire Support for Brim Extension

in one-half inch of the brim edge, with the long stitch on the upper side, cut the velvet off even with the brim edge and overcast it all around. Treat the velvet on the under

92

side of the brim in the same manner. Be sure and trim the velvet even with the brim edge, for if it projects ever so little, and then is overcast, it will be lumpy, and show through the binding.

Figure 2 shows the round binding. This is the narrowest and most economical binding in use. It is made of a bias strip, which is slightly stretched, and sewed on the upper side of the brim near its edge. The stitches should be one-quarter of an inch long on the upper side ,and small on the underbrim. Bring the velvet over the brim edge, turn in the raw edge and blindstitch it down. This makes a truly round binding. Its width can be gauged by measuring the velvet on the upper and lower brim edge, and adding to that the turn in on each edge of the binding. The round binding is only recommended where economy is the object.

LESSON XVII

French Design Work

The plain manner of manipulating velvets has now been carefully considered, and the next step is to learn some of the more fancy methods.

French design work consists of sewing different patterns into the velvet, and allowing the proper fulness for their perfect development.

The first design shown in Figure 1, is called the chrysanthemum pattern, and Figure 2 shows the tracing done on the wrong side of the velvet, to be followed in the stitching to produce this effect. Take an ordinary sized glass tumbler, turn it bottom side up, and draw·your pencil around its rim as it lies on the wrong side of the velvet. Put a dot in the center of the circle, and from it draw circular lines, as shown in the diagram, watching that the line next to the circle made by the tumbler, shall be properly spaced. Take a fine short needle, and No. 50 thread the color of the velvet. Begin in the center and secure the thread firmly, as the gathering depends upon this fastening. Sew only three short stitches at a time, following the design, and after the second round is made, draw up the thread as tight as you can. From this point on do the gathering less and less tightly until the outer circle is completed. The center will then stand up like a cone as it has to be drawn so very tight in the center in order that there shall be any fulness on the outer edge. When the gathering is properly arranged a small hole is punched in the buckram, upon which the velvet is to be placed, and the top of the cone is pulled through the hole and given a slight twist. This arranges the radiating lines of the gathers more gracefully. Stick pins around the outer circle, just as it should lie on the buckram, take your needle, secure the center in its place and then tack down the outer circle. If any one part sticks up too much near the center, stitch it in place in the folds of the gathering, so it will not show. Press a refractory place down on the buckram, if it needs it, and take a stitch which must always point toward the center. Sewing crossgrain would be ruinous.

For a flat brim, or the upstanding brim of a turban, eight designs will be found sufficient. One in the front, one in the back, two on the sides, at right angles, and finally, one between each of all these. That makes the eight. They should be on

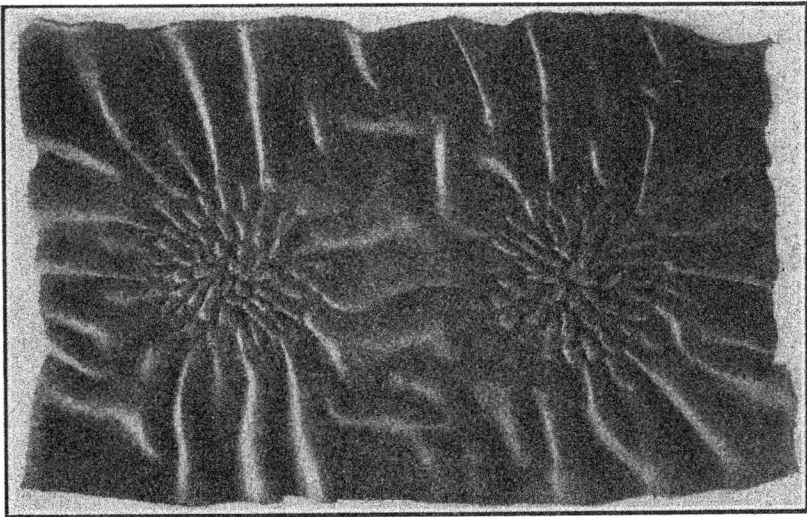

No. 1. Chrysanthemum design.

the upper side of a flat brim, or the outer side of a turned up brim. In velvet we allow one and one-quarter of its length for all gathering. This will be found sufficient for the design work. Measure around the edge of your brim, and it will require one and one-quarter times that amount in length to go around it. It should be a bias piece, as wide as the upper

and lower brim, with one-quarter added. The velvet is one
continuous piece, from the headsize over the upper side of the
brim, down over the brim edge, over the underbrim to the

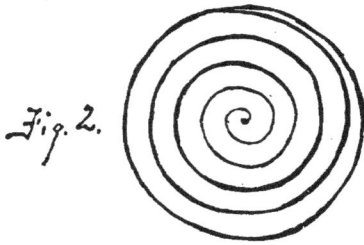

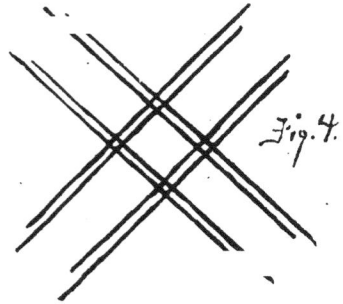

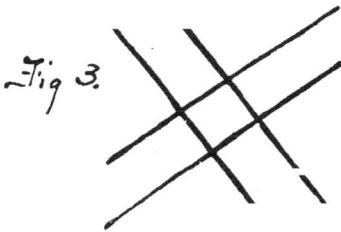

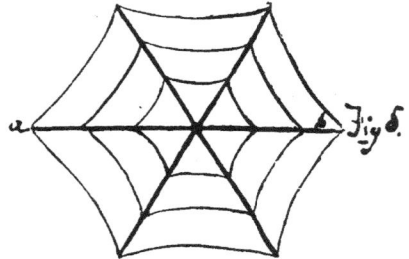

Fig. 2.

Fig. 4.

Fig 3.

Fig 5.

headsize again. So with one-quarter added for the length and
one-quarter added to the width you have the dimensions of
the piece of velvet required for the brim. It will probably take
two pieces of the bias velvet to make the brim. Sew them
together in two diagonal seams so that it will make a circle
of the velvet. Mark your first design for the front, and it
should be in the middle of one of the bias pieces, so that the
seams will be on the sides. Double the velvet in two, lengthwise. Take one for the upper and the other for the lower
side of the brim. Allow enough for a seam at the headsize,
and put the designs equally distant from where this seam will
come, to the brim edge. Space the eight designs, sew them,
put them on the brim, and the fulled velvet between the designs, and around them must be caught with the smallest of

stitches from the under side, to make the velvet lie in graceful contour. It is easier to determine this by sticking pins where later the stitches will be taken. Gather the velvet at the head-size, on the upper and lower side and stitch it in place.

A round or oblong crown is covered with a single piece of velvet, the dimensions of which are determined by measuring the crown from front to back, and from side to side, and adding one-quarter to this measure.

One design is made exactly in the center of the top crown. Six are grouped around this one, so their outer rim is as far away as the diameter of the design. If the crown is very large, six more may be added, the same distance below the first row, as it was from the central design. The figures of the second row should alternate with those of the first row.

The making of such a hat necessitates the use of a finishing or milliner's fold at the base of the crown. This is one of the most beautiful and artistic effects known to millinery. The chrysanthemum design can be made of any size. A crown top may be completely covered with one design. In such a case, do not forget that the center must be drawn up so much more by the gathering, in order to have any fulness on the outer edge. If the crown top is oblong, add a few curved lines at the front and back, coming into the circle, at their beginning and ending.

Chrysanthemums no larger than a half dollar, may cover a crown top, making one in the center, and grouping six about it to conform to the shape of the crown top. This can be used with a plain side crown, which would be a separate piece. These designs can be sewed on crinoline, and used in soft crown tops, but they are not so effective as when sewed to firm buckram.

Beside the chrysanthemum pattern we have the crossbar and double crossbar, shown in Figure 3 and Figure 4. The lines in the diagrams simply denote how the seams should be placed and can be laid off on the velvet, by a white thread, in long stitches on the right side. The seam itself is a double in the velvet, made on the line of the white thread on the right side. Begin on the edge of the double, slope gently downward until the seam is one-eighth of an inch wide. Sew it at that width until near its termination, where it is sloped upward to the edge of the double again.

Be careful in making the seams across each other, that you do not sew through the gathering threads, or they could not be drawn up. After the design is all seamed, draw the seams up, just enough to ruffle the velvet slightly and sufficient to make the designs stand out clearly, then thread the loose ends of the seams, and run the needle through to the wrong side, and fasten securely. The fulled velvet, about the designs, should be disposed of, as in the first pattern. These designs can be made large or small, as desired.

The last pattern shows the spider web in Figure 5. To make it, you first determine where you want the center of the web. Place a pin at this point, double the velvet in a straight line, so that the center pin will be as nearly in the middle of the double as possible.

Determine how large you want the web, and place two pins equally distant, from the center pin, one on each side, and both along the double. This will give the diameter of the web. Place four pins, two on each side of the double, so that they shall be equally distant from each other, and the two pins placed along the double, with the center pin. They must also be the same distance from the center pin as those on the double. These six straight lines, radiating from the center, to the six pins, should be marked with white thread, in long stitches on the right side. Mark off three slightly curved lines, between each two straight ones, as shown in the diagrams, and stitch them with the white thread also.

98

Commence with a fine needle, and fine thread, the color of the velvet, and seam along the first double from A to B, beginning with the edge of the velvet, and getting wider, gradually, until at the center the seam should be one-eighth of an inch wide, then decrease from the center to B and draw up the seam, so that it lightly waves the velvet. Fasten the end securely, even with the edge of the double. Sew the other four straight lines, separately, commencing at the outer edge and ending in one-eighth of an inch seam in the center.

The curved crossing lines, between the six just sewed should be slightly gathered, each one separately, and the whole design pinned down to the foundation of the hat, and then stitched in place. The curved seams are then chain-stitched, in heavy embroidery silk, in a contrasting color to the velvet, or some tint or shade of the same color. The center of the web is finished in a jewel, or with beads, spangles, jet or anything that taste may suggest. These webs may be made large enough to cover the top of a crown, and can be elongated in design to fit the crown of that shape.

All of these designs must be sewed with short stitches, and exact work done in their embellishment and mounting.

Hand-made appliqué motifs on an odd turban

LESSON XVIII

Five Different Crowns

As Fashion comes and goes, there are five shapes of the crown, that appear periodically, as something startlingly new.

The first is the Gainsborough proper; by that I mean the crown shown in the Gainsborough portraits. This crown is straight on the sides, circular in form, and flat on the top. It is always a high crown, but its proportions vary somewhat although the usual width of the side crown is three-quarters the diameter of the top. Thus, if the crown top has a diameter of 8 inches, the height of the side crown would be three-fourths of 8 inches, which equals 6 inches.

The true Gainsborough hat is not supposed to come down on the head, as is often the style for years together, but it is perched jauntily on the side of the head, the wide straight brim given sweeping and graceful curves, and the whole structure loaded with plumes, artistically placed in flowing lines.

The top crown is cut in circular form of any required diameter, in the same manner as the Gainsborough brim. It is wired around its circumference, even with the edge. The wiring is done on the rough side of the buckram, leaving the smooth side for contact with the velvet, or any fabric covering. The side crown is cut in a continuous straight strip, of equal width, and is closed by an overlap of two inches at the back. It must be fitted so it will exactly go around the crown top, and neither squeeze the top nor leave the slightest opening. Close the overlap of the side crown, with long stitches, wire the headsize, on the inside, even with the edge, then wire the upper edge just the width of the wire below the edge itself,

The original Gainsborough Hat

so that when the crown top with its wire is put within the side crown the wire of the crown top will rest on the wire of the side crown, as upon a shelf. Next, stitch the crown top and side crown together, with long stitches driven through from the crown top to the side crown, going under both wires and holding them together. Repeated stitches of this kind make an overcast all about the crown.

Curving the Crown Top

Sometimes the slightest curve is desired in the crown top. This can be effected by cutting out a piece of sheet wadding the size of the crown top and pulling off a thin layer on the edge all around and placing the side that has been torn next to the crown top. This makes the least bit of fulness and takes away the severity of the straight lines.

The velvet or fabric is placed with the bias to the front of the crown top, and stretched and pinned on like the Gainsborough brim, extending down on the side crown for one-third of an inch. After it is pinned perfectly smooth it is stitched around on the side crown far enough from the edge of the velvet so that it will not ravel, and yet not so near the top that the stitching will show, when the side crown velvet is put on. Make the stitch one-third of an inch long on the right side and very short on the wrong side. See that the stitch on the right side holds down the goods without any puckers or they will later show in a bunch through the fabric of the side crown.

Cut a bias strip of velvet wide enough to cover the side crown, turn in ½ inch on either edge. You must also allow for the stretching of the velvet, which lessens its width. After one edge of the velvet is cut on the bias it can be stretched and pinned about the side crown, to get some idea of the desired width before the other bias edge is cut from the piece of goods.

Turn in half inch at the top edge of the bias piece; commence in the back of the side crown, pin it down, and stretch it about the crown top and exactly even with it. There are two methods of closing it in the back of the side crown. If the velvet is sufficiently wide, cut off the ends square, and turn them in one-half inch on either end. Turn down the ½ inch coming around the crown top, that is immediately in the back, *after* the ends are turned in, so that the lap-under on the ends will not show at the crown top after the side crown is closed at the back. This closing is done with blind stitching, commencing at the top of the same, piercing the needle through the buckram and back, so that the stitching may never slip down. The bottom of the side crown is finished by turning under the velvet into the headsize of the crown and stitching it with a fine needle and thread, barely above the bottom wire, making the long stitch on the inside of the crown and the small one on the outside. The stitches should be one-half inch long on the inside and the smallest that will hold the fabric on the right side. This finishes the true Gainsborough crown.

The Puritan Crown

The second form of crown is the Puritan, and is very like the Gainsborough, only the side crown is sloping slightly, hence making a smaller crown top. This is sometimes called the "sugar loaf" crown, as it has the exact shape of the cone, in which that commodity used to be sold, except that the top is cut squarely off.

Any picture of the Pilgrims will give a vivid idea of this peculiar headpiece, and as instructions have been given for cutting a sloping side crown. the Puritan shape can be easily reproduced by slashing the side crown of the Gainsborough from its upper edge nearly to the headsize and overlapping. After getting the proper slope it can be cut from buckram in one continuous piece, and a flat top can be fitted into its upper opening.

The Puritan crown is sometimes made with a flat oval top, and is used with all shapes of brims.

The third of these crowns is the beretta, which was primarily taken from the priest's cap of that name. It is usually cut in four pieces and put together with a heavy cord in the seams. The top is nearly flat, and can be brought back to the headsize with gathers or after the top is of sufficient size the four pieces can be sloped in so they will exactly fit the headsize, where they are sewed into a narrow band about the head. The true beretta is not very large on the top, but in its modifications for millinery it is corded or not, and is sometimes cut plain and round, and either gathered or plaited into the headsize. We have the artist's beretta made this way, and slightly pulled to one side. This crown can be made with the head band, making a complete hat that way, or it can be used on a brim of any size or form.

The fourth shape is the Tam o' Shanter, which is ordinarily cut in two round disks, in one of which is cut out the headsize. The two are put together with a heavy covered cord between the edges, or it can be made of one larger round piece, turned under on itself and plaited or gathered into the headsize, when there is no difference between it and the beretta but a name.

The mortar board is the fifth form of crown. This, in its most severe form, used by scholars, is a square piece of pasteboard, covered with cloth on both sides, and a long drooping tassel, on one side of the point, which is directly in front and seems disposed to cloud the vision of one eye. This board is attached to a round close-fitting skull cap at its top. The fastening is sufficiently strong, so the four points cannot vary in position.

For the millinery trade this crown is varied, so that a square piece of buckram the required size of the board may have a round center cut out of it so that the narrowest parts of the buckram will be only two inches wide. In many cases the four corners are reinforced with a triangular piece of buckram and a small wire, called lace wire, is sewed around the four sides of the outer edge. This braces it, but yet leaves it very pliable.

The cloth stretched over this frame may be divided into four equal parts, starting in the center, and running to the four points. It may be corded in the seams, and instead of being rigidly flat it may be rounded slightly toward the center. The buckram will hold the corners firmly and a bias strip of the goods may be sewed around the edge of the board, with or without a cord, as desired. The bias piece can then be drawn up to fit a head band, leaving the bias piece wider opposite the points of the board, and gradually narrowing down in the spaces between, so that the bias piece will pull equally into the headsize. When this is worn the head will make it curved over the top, while the points stand out well defined. It can be used with or without a brim.

By noting these different suggestions for crowns many and varied effects can be produced.

Increasing the height of a shallow crown by trimming.

LESSON XIX

Draping Crowns and Velvet on Concave Surface

Periodically the smooth velvet on the crowns is wrinkled into strange and mysterious shapes. Sometimes it is but little elevated above the buckram foundation, and at others it is given a prodigious height, at the back of the crown top, on either side or both, or in front.

These humps and valleys must have some foundation for support, and they must be disposed in an artistic manner, or it will prove the step from the sublime to the ridiculous. In the illustration we see exemplified various ways of supporting the folds.

When fashion justifies the elevation of the back of the crown top, and also dictates that it should extend slightly backward from its base, the wire support portrayed will hold it firmly in place. It is necessary to first line the crown with a strip of buckram 3 inches wide, extending from the headsize in front to the headsize in the back. When the curve comes, at the commencement of the crown top, cut the buckram strip from each side, leaving only a small space in the center. Let the slit be in conformity to the curve, and when the buckram is pressed in place the slit pieces will overlap each other, so that this extra piece of buckram will lie snugly against the crown for its whole length. Stitch the bracing piece firmly to the crown and you have a firm foundation for the supports. These wire supports are made of one piece, and the wire is crossed at the base and spread out in two triangular flanges like duck's feet, forming a substantial foundation.

The larger wire support can be made pointed as in the

illustration, or it may be broad across the top and set parallel to the width of the crown top, coming down to the base, with the two wire sides of equal length.

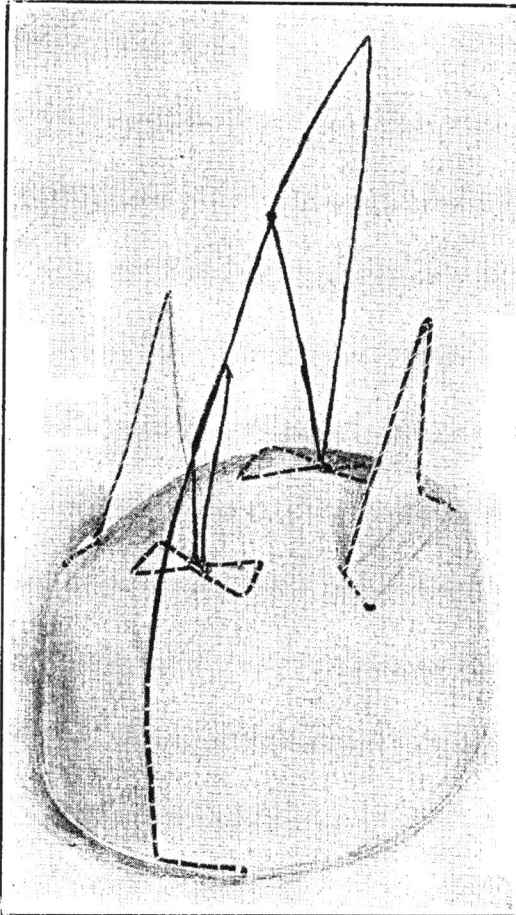

Building up the crown for Draping.

A lesser wire support can be placed midway of the crown top, and one connecting wire brought from the back support over the middle one, and drawn down over the front of the crown, being even with the crown top, where it merges into the side crown.

Other supports are made of buckram and wired on the upstanding edges. One-half inch, including the wire ends, is turned outward at the base to conform to the shape of the crown top, where it is desired to use it.

If the supports are made as shown in the illustration the velvet can be taken where it is cut square across, and the bias corner can be turned in for 3 or 4 inches, and the two sides on the straight brought together like a cornucopia, and it can then be slipped over the wire standard at the back of the crown. This brings the bias down the middle of the draping on the crown top, and this main rib may be made in curves. The side supports will hold another fold of the fulness. These folds should be carefully arranged so that they converge at the front and hold them in place by pins, thrust straight in through the crown top.

About the hardest thing in millinery is to give a perfectly flowing and careless effect, when the goods must be so secured that it will hold in place against wear and weather.

After the draping is finished, and the pins placed, not always bringing the velvet in contact with the crown, take a long needle and fine cotton thread, the color of the velvet, and beginning on the under side of the crown top stitch through the velvet at the places pinned, being very careful not to pull the velvet down when returning the needle into the crown top. Many places the thread will have to be carried along parallel to the crown top in order to secure the folds exactly in place and not pull them down. Especially is this the case when coming to the main rib of the draping. The needle must go under the long connecting wire, but never make a draw in the velvet. The stitch on the right side at all times is the smallest possible and becomes invisible, as it sinks into the pile of the velvet.

103

The side crown can be laid on smooth or in folds or with a shirred upstanding edge and various forms of shirring down the whole side. Anything that taste may suggest or the contour of the face justify can be used. If one possesses very little originality one may select some prettily draped crown and copy it. Such suggestions can always be found in a good millinery magazine.

A smart and even way to drape a crown is to lay five plaits at the front of the crown top. Let each plait be one-half inch deep and lay them all in the same direction so that they barely come in contact with each other and do not overlap. Drape the plaits so that they widen apart as they reach the middle of the crown top, and at that point secure them with pins stuck straight in between the plaits. At the back of the crown top make five similar plaits, only in the opposite direction. Pin them exactly in place, as the front ones are, remove the pins in the center of the crown top, and you will find that the reversing of the plaits makes a fine fluted effect. The plaits must not be drawn too tight, and a few fine stitches will hold them in place. The side crown can be treated the same as in the case of the high draped crown top.

There is no end to the variety of designs that can be produced by the use of supports, wires, shirrings, folds and draped goods.

Many shapes present a concave surface on the upper or lower brim. The velvet must be placed upon the concave surface, be it up or down, before the other side of the brim is covered. Let us take a tricorne, for instance.

Place the bias point of the goods at the front point of the brim and on the upper side. Let the velvet at the front be sufficiently far from the bias point so that when the velvet is pressed down to conform to the shape it will still reach the brim edge at all points and allow one-half inch beyond it. This must be done very carefully. Next pin the velvet to the front point and with forefinger and thumb of each hand work the velvet down, stretching it on the bias, either lengthwise or crosswise as required to fit the form. Pin the brim edge and thrust pins straight through the velvet and buckram elsewhere. Only place a small portion of the velvet at a time. Then take a small needle and fine cotton thread, the color of the velvet, and starting on the wrong side stitch through to the right side and back again with as small a stitch as will hold the goods to the buckram. The stitch should be invisible when the velvet is brushed at the completion of the stitching. Stitch back and forth across the front point, making the stitches one-half inch apart and each row one-half inch distance from the last. All the time keep fitting the velvet, and if any one place "blisters" so as not to touch the buckram and put in an extra stitch to hold it down.

Work the velvet toward the back, and after it progresses enough on each side to begin to cover the headsize, cut out the headsize just that far and no farther. Nothing is more deceiving than the exact place of the headsize, and it can only be cut out safely little by little as the fitting proceeds.

As the back is reached, the velvet in the headsize will stand up in a ridge, getting higher toward the back. At last the velvet must be brought together at the back and cut in a straight gash from the headsize to the brim edge, allowing one-half inch on either side for a turn-in.

The remaining part of the headsize is now cut away, the back turned in and blindstitched together, and the final fine stitching done to hold down the velvet in the back.

Velvet can be fitted in this manner over almost any

shape, widening or narrowing the velvet in the bias of the goods.

Lastly, the velvet is taken over the brim edge and stitched down to the rough binding as in the Gainsborough brim. The velvet of the underbrim is pinned in place at the brim edge and can be fitted smoothly by pulling the bias of the goods. Baste it with fine needle and thread, about one and one-half inches from the brim edge. The velvet should now be trimmed away, leaving one-half inch projecting beyond the brim edge. This is turned in even with the brim edge and blindstitched to the upper brim.

A dip in the crown top or a concave side crown can be covered in the same way as the brim, only in the crown top the fitting begins in the center.

Hat manufacturers employ a colorless millinery adhesive for applying the velvet, securing it over a form or mold with great pressure. The old-fashioned glues often injured the pile of the velvet, and it could not be raised without loosening the velvet from the frame. The new improved millinery adhesives are wonderful time savers in the milliner's workroom, but in spite of their perfection they are a perilous thing in the hands of the amateur, as one "smutch" of the fluid on the fingers or too much of it under the velvet is apt to produce a pressed down spot, that to try to correct is to make worse. Before attempting to use the adhesive, it is not only advisable but absolutely necessary to experiment, taking the more tedious method of sewing the hat until one has become sufficiently conversant with the use of the adhesives.

LESSON XX
Transparent Hats

The first of the transparent hats to be considered is the chiffon hat, that is, a hat made of chiffon folds. The initial step is therefore the cutting of the folds. Lay the chiffon out straight on a table, with the end of the piece towards you. Take this end and fold it along the selvage of the left hand side. This gives a true bias on the right hand side. See that it does not pull out longer than its natural width on the bias line.

Take the bias on the right hand side and fold it back on the piece of chiffon until the bias comes even with the farthest point, where the chiffon lies with double thickness. The chiffon is now in one fold of four thicknesses and the fold must be of uniform width, but its ends will be irregular. Again, take the bias on the right hand and fold it to the left, until it is even with the first bias that was made. Repeat this process unil the fold is of the required width, which is usually about 3 inches. Be sure that this folding is done exactly, so no part has stretched, or it will come out uneven when the folds are cut.

Take a fine needle and fine thread and stitch down the middle of the folded piece of chiffon with stitches two inches long. Watch that the stitches do not misplace the folds. Now take the scissors and cut directly across the fold any width desired, and when it is unwound it will be a bias strip of equal width all its way, if the process has been properly managed. The selvage is always cut off and the strips are sewed together with a very small seam, which is pressed open with the fingers. Fine thread is used entirely in making a chiffon hat. After the seams are sewed, pull the whole piece *across its width* and roll it up very lightly, when it is ready for use.

Cutting Chiffon

The theory of cutting chiffon can be exemplified with a piece of paper, which may be folded across its bias, and folded again and again according to directions. It can be basted down and cut across, and one can more readily see the process because the paper does not stretch, as the chiffon surely does. The chiffon hat is made on a wire frame, which is covered with a plain piece of chiffon. First on the underbrim, where it is pinned in place, and overcast around the brim edge, and headsize, extending over the brim edge wire for one-quarter of an inch. Then the upper brim is covered in the same manner, making two thicknesses of the chiffon for a foundation for the folds. The first fold is put around the brim edge as a binding, extending equally on the upper brim and the lower. This is stitched to its place, with equal stitches on both sides, and as near the raw edge as it can without fraying out.

The next fold is doubled its full length, and be very careful not to stretch it lengthwise. It is laid on the upper side so it will project over the brim edge about one-eighth of an inch. Stitch in place along the raw edge, with equal stitches on both sides, and one-quarter of an inch in length. The next fold is put on the under brim in the same manner as the one on the upper brim, and the stitching must come exactly in the same place as that of the upper brim. The next fold is put on the upper brim, so that its edge will nicely cover the sewing on the raw edge of the first double fold. The raw edge of this last fold is sewed on like the others, and the next fold is placed right under it on the underbrim, so the sewing of the two folds will come in the same place, and this process is continued to the headsize. (See illustration.)

When a fold is begun the ends are turned in before it is folded, and when the fold terminates it is finished in the same manner, so the turned in ends come together in the back. A constant endeavor must be maintained to keep the raw edge of each fold from stretching, in fact, it should be held the smallest bit *full,* to allow the doubled edge to curve around freely, to conform to the curve of the brim.

If the under side of the brim is to be covered with a shirred facing, only the upper folds needs to be put on, one after another. If the folds of the upper brim are *narrow,* they are sometimes made in a continuous strip, beginning a little to the right of the exact back, going completely around the brim edge to the place of beginning, where it should slope gradually upward toward the headsize to make the second round, and the extra thickness of the first fold, that will show under the beginning of the second, should be cut away.

If the upper and lower brims are both covered with folds, the slight projections beyond the brim edge should be tie-stitched together about every two inches with very fine thread, so that those outer folds will not *flap* in the wind. Take a small stitch to the left, on the under fold, and through only one thickness. Exactly above it take a small stitch to the right in he upper fold, and tie them together, but not so tightly that it will draw.

The crown is covered with two thicknesses of chiffon, to correspond with the brim, but in this case both thicknesses are put on the outside of the wire form. The crown top is pinned in place and overcast. The side crown is fitted by a straight piece of chiffon, doubled, if the side crown is straight. If the side crown slopes slightly the doubled chiffon can be drawn tightly around it from the front, where it should be pinned to the back, where it will end slightly on the bias and where

114

it will have to be overlapped and stitched down. Then stitch it in place where the crown top begins and overcast the headsize.

If the side crown slopes more than can be taken smoothly up by pulling the chiffon toward the back, cut out a paper pattern to fit the side crown, and lay it on the doubled chiffon, so that the doubled edge of the chiffon will be at the top, and extending beyond it, where the upper edge is curved. Cut out the bottom, allowing an extra half inch to turn under at the headsize; cut the ends so they will overlap.

Leave the doubled edge of the chiffon until the chiffon is pinned around the crown top, then the extra projection can be cut away. Close the overlap in the back, stitch around the crown top and overcast about the headsize.

Applying Chiffon Folds

The folds are put on the crown the same as on the upper brim, beginning at the headsize in the back, and ending with the gathering of the fold into a round rosette for a finish at the very tip of the crown, or again, if the fold is sufficiently narrow, the crown can be covered in one continuous piece, going round and round the crown, and finishing with the rosette.

Beautiful effects can be produced by varying the chiffon folds with transparent braids. A fine or fancy straw hat is sometimes given an underbrim lining of chiffon folds. In such a case a crinoline lining is cut exactly to fit. This is covered with plain chiffon and the edge bound with a chiffon fold, and then the succeeding folds laid on one after another as before described until the headsize is reached. The entire lining is then pinned on the underbrim and stitched to place on its edge with the stilting stitch. When stitched at the headsize the lining is complete.

115

Maline hats are made in the same way as the chiffon, only the folds of maline are made of straight strips turned in from both edges of the length until they meet. Then the outer

The
various
stages of
covering
hat brim
with
folds.

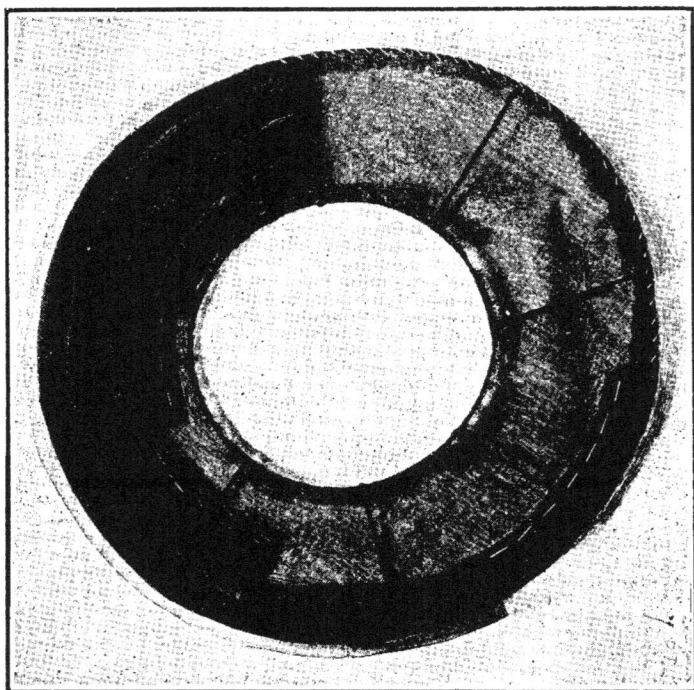

edges are folded together, and a fine basting run along the middle of the fold, when it is ready for use. This folding gives four thicknesses of maline. Frequently a gathering thread is required on the upper edge, where the sides come together. Maline folds can be used with braids also, or with bands of fancy straw leaves, as shown in fancy braid sewing.

Lace hats can be made on wire frames, covered smoothly with chiffon or maline. If the lace is narrow, it can be slightly fulled by pulling up the draw string on its upper edge and sew it from the brim edge to the headsize, each round slightly overlapping the last enough to hide the sewing. The lace should project a little over the brim edge, and it is preferable to only put the lace on the upper brim and finish the under-brim with a shirred lining of chiffon, maline or net. A crown can also be made of the lace.

In metallic laces it is often desirable to have no frame covering under the lace. The frame should match the lace in color, that is, if the lace should be silver, the frame should be made of silver wire, and if the lace should be of gold, the frame should be made of gilded wire. When these wires can not be obtained, a common white wire frame can be treated to a liquid wash that will produce a silver or gold effect and can be bought at any drug store. If some certain color is wanted, a white wire frame can be changed to any shade or tint by mixing tube paint and gasoline and painting it, or, better still, dipping it in the dye. The lace, too, can be colored, but it must be immersed, all at one time, and the paint and gasoline must be thoroughly mixed and poured off into a second vessel, so there will be no sediment to produce spots. It takes very little of the tube paint and considerable of the gasoline, and it must *never* be used near a fire.

If the metallic lace is wide enough to reach from the headsize to the brim edge, gather it into the headsize with sufficient fulness so that it will lie smoothly at the brim edge. Stitch it to the headsize wire, and again at the brim edge, letting any scallops project beyond the edge wire. If the metallic lace is not wide enough to cover the whole brim, see that a wire is so placed that it will meet the gathering string after the brim edge is pinned in place. If it only takes two widths of the lace to reach the headsize they can be overlapped at this middle wire, but if the lace has to be pieced out toward the headsize after the brim edge is secured and the gathering of the first row of the lace has been fastened to the wire between the brim edge and the headsize, the wire can be covered with a narrow finishing fold of velvet or satin.

The crown top may be covered with straight pieces of the lace, running from front to back, with the two plain edges of the lace coming together across the middle of the crown top. These plain edges can be covered with a narrow finishing fold of silk or satin also.

The side crown may be made with the scalloped edge of the lace standing up around the crown top and finished at the headsize with a finishing fold. If it should require two widths of the lace for the side crown they can be managed in the same manner as in the brim.

A shirred net hat can be sewed directly on the wire frame. The strips may be cut crosswise, bias, or along the length of the net. In the last case we get the smallest amount of seams. The strip for the brim should be three times as long as the brim edge and as wide as the brim, and any projection beyond the brim edge, multiplied by two, for the net has to go both on the upper and lower brim. Then allow two inches extra for the turn in at the headsize, one inch for the upper brim and one inch for the lower brim.

Suppose it is desirable to have the net extend in a frill for one inch beyond the edge wire, and that the brim is five inches wide; then we will cut a strip fourteen inches wide, two inches for the extension beyond the edge wire, ten inches to cover the brim proper, and two inches to turn in at the headsize. Double the strip of net lengthwise and run a gathering thread around it one inch from the doubled edge and open out the two thicknesses, and put the net around the brim, one thickness above and one below the wires, and the frill extending one inch beyond the edge wire. Divide the fulness into four equal parts, pinning the net in front, at the back and at the two sides, and dispose the gathers equally. Draw up the thread and fasten it. Now pin the two thicknesses of net together, just within the brim edge wire. Run a stitching in the net and through both thicknesses, close to the brim edge wire, and after the complete circle is made draw up the thread and make it fast. This encases the brim edge wire in the net, and each wire may be similarly treated by running a gathering thread on both sides of it. This process is shown in the illustration.

At the headsize, gather the net on the top and under brim separately, and stitch them together afterward. The crown is covered with a strip as long as three times the distance around the headsize, and as wide as the measure from the crown tip to the headsize, plus one inch for a turn in. Sew the strip together in a small felled seam, and turn in one-quarter of an inch on one edge, and gather it very tight, as near the doubled edge as possible. Sew it to the centre of the crown top with the seam of the net in the back.

Put a gathering thread where the crown top begins and another at the headsize. If any more gatherings are desired, let them come directly over the extra wires on the crown top and the side crown. Dispose the fulness evenly and baste the net to the wires with small stitches on the right side, and stitches one-half inch long on the wrong side, but make the thread encircle the wire by taking one little stitch *above* the wire and the next *below* it, so that the shirring will stay in place.

With laces, malines, chiffons and transparent straws of all varieties of quality and colors, wondrous designs can be produced that delight the artistic eye.

LESSON XXI

Transparent Brims and Brim Extensions

Transparent brims and brim extensions come in style periodically as the wheel of Fashion turns on its round. The transparent sprung brim is generally made of maline or chiffon. If the uncovered wire is used for the brim edge, it can be cut to any sized circle desired and the ends fastened with a metal clamp, which can be purchased with the wire. Use the pliers in pressing down the clamp, after the wire ends are inserted, and then cut a wire headsize. It is best to cut the maline on the straight. Take the piece of maline, fold it over on its length to twice the width desired for the brim (measuring from the headsize to the brim edge) and cut it off long enough to go around the edge wire, very tight, and lap over an inch.

Put the middle of this strip around the edge wire, pulling it firmly into place, and where it laps over stick in a pin, near the brim edge, to hold the ends together.

Be careful that the maline does not slip on the edge wire. Now draw the fulness of the maline to the headsize, keeping each layer of the four thicknesses equally taut. Run a strong thread through the maline, as near the headsize as possible. Let the stitches be small, to avoid wrinkles. Draw the thread up and the maline will straighten out flat. Fasten the thread so its circle will be complete, and the maline smooth and firm. If maline seems refractory and too stiff to lay smoothly about the headsize, the least touch of steam at that point will elongate the holes of the mesh and make it spread out flat. Be very careful not to use too much moisture, and be sure it only touches about the headsize. Cut away the superfluous maline in the lap-over, from the headsize to the brim edge, so that there will be only one inch lap-over left, and do not attempt to turn it in, for it will never show if the edge is left raw, and it would show by the extra thickness if it were turned in.

Place the headsize wire on the upper side of the brim, and overcast it to the maline, using small stitches, and keeping the fulness of the maline as smooth as possible. Turn the extra

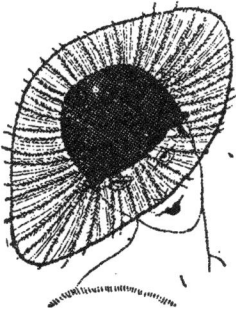

A smart hat, always in style, and especially desirable for evening or restaurant wear. The interesting feature is the irregular brim of some sheer fabric shirred to wire. The trimming of fine strands of plumage may be replaced by flowers or any preferred garniture

maline up into the headsize and the brim is now ready for the crown.

If the uncovered wire is used for the brim edge it is usually finished with a round binding (see Lesson on Bindings) of silk, satin or velvet. If the binding is not to be used, the wire of the brim edge should correspond in color with the maline. If a white covered wire is used and tied with covered tie wire, the whole can be colored any tint or shade, with tube paint and gasoline.

A transparent brim extension is usually put on a wire frame before the braid or cloth covering is arranged. Suppose the brim is composed of three wires, namely, the brim edge, the headsize, and the wire between these two. Make the circle for the transparent extension to lay outside of the three wires, and as far beyond the brim edge as desired.

Fold and cut the maline to go around the extension the same as in the transparent brim, making the strip wide enough to go over the extension wire and to reach up on both the outer and under sides to the middle wire of the frame proper. Gather the maline at the middle wire of brim and overcast it to that wire and also to the edge wire of the frame. All four thicknesses of the maline may be placed on top of the wire brim, or the brim may be slipped in between these thicknesses, leaving two above and two below. In this case the maline is gathered twice, once above the second wire of the brim and again below it.

After the extension is adjusted very tight and smooth, the braid, crêpe or silk for the wire brim proper can be sewed on.

Transparent brims and brim extensions can be made of net, maline, chiffon or lace. Sometimes a transparent brim edge is made of a wavy hair braid, prettily scalloped, or a lace edge may hang straight down.

If a transparent extension is desired on a pressed straw, there are ordinarily a few rounds of milan forming a brim revers on the upper side of the brim, which can readily be ripped off, the transparent gathering sewed down, and the milan circle replaced to hide it.

Some milliners use four wires, fastened on the headsize and extending to the brim edge for additional supports for a transparent brim. In such a case, two thicknesses of the maline go above the wires and two below them, and two gathering threads are required at the headsize.

The brim extension is made in a different manner by extending four of the eight wires, fastened on the headsize of the wire brim, until they are clamped down on the edge of the extension. This gives four wire supports to the outer circle, but detracts from its beauty somewhat.

Various and effective are the many conceits made from transparent and diaphanous materials, and for grace and beauty they have no equal.

A Famous
Millinery
Classic

The Lady
with the Muff

by

Mme. Vigée
Lebrun

123

LESSON. XXII

Bows and Other Fancies

The Single Alsatian Bow

The Alsatian bow, see Fig. 1, is the foundation bow of all bows. This basic factor, with its myriad variations, has filled the world with the art productions in that line.

Take one yard of 4-inch ribbon and fishtail both ends. This is done by folding the ribbon in the middle lengthwise, at the ends only, making the selvages come together. Next bend the middle of the end out to the selvage so that the upper edge of the end will be parallel and just even with the selvage. Cut across the diagonal double and it gives the notched effect called fishtailing. If the diagonal cut is slightly curved outward it will relieve the eye of the severity of the straight line and give a better effect. If the ribbon is the same on both sides an Alsatian bow is always constructed like the letter "Z." It is divided into three parts, one end is laid on the table, then the ribbon is folded back upon the first layer, and the last third is folded back over the second layer. It is then adjusted so that the fold of the ribbon at the ends will come half across the fishtail, and when this is done the whole three thicknesses are doubled over and creased all together, right across the middle of their length. This will mark the three places for plaits.

Unfold the ribbon and take the marked line for plaiting nearest to the fishtail of one end. Hold the ribbon firmly in the left hand at this place with the thumb on the upper side of the ribbon and the fingers on the under side. With the thumb of the right hand make a small plait and push it between the thumb and fingers of the left hand. After the plait ribbon is different on the two sides, the folds, after plaiting, are arranged a little differently, as shown in the illustration No. 3, so as to keep one side uppermost all the while.

The center of the bow is plaited very fine, and sewed down at the back, on the middle of the bow. Bring the ribbon over on the right side and reverse the plaiting, where it will go under again on to the back of the bow. As each plait is made, run the middle finger of the right hand up from underneath, making the fluted effect for the bow center shown in Fig. 2.

Fasten this end underneath, tie stitch the loop and end on either side of the center, so they will hold in proper place and the bow is done. All tie stitching in bows is done at half the length of the loops. If it is placed too near the end of the loop, it gives a stiff expression to the whole bow.

Two of these single Alsatian bows, without the center pieces, are used to construct the double Alsatian bow. They are laid side by side, and one edge of the plaiting in the middle of each is sewed to the other, so that the center will lie flat. Then a center piece is put on, as in the single Alsatian bow, and the loops and ends are arranged and tie stitched, so they will alternate. This completes the bow, which is in itself enough trimming for any large sun hat.

These Alsatian bows can be made of any width ribbon, so that the same proportions are observed and they may be used for hats, dresses or the hair.

One more Alsatian bow should be mentioned, that is, the standing Alsatian. This, together with the single, double and fancy Alsatian, gives a fair idea of these bows; and they form models, whose variations are numerous and delightful.

The standing Alsatian is made of a single Alsatian bow, with a loop made of 10 inches of ribbon, and an end seven and

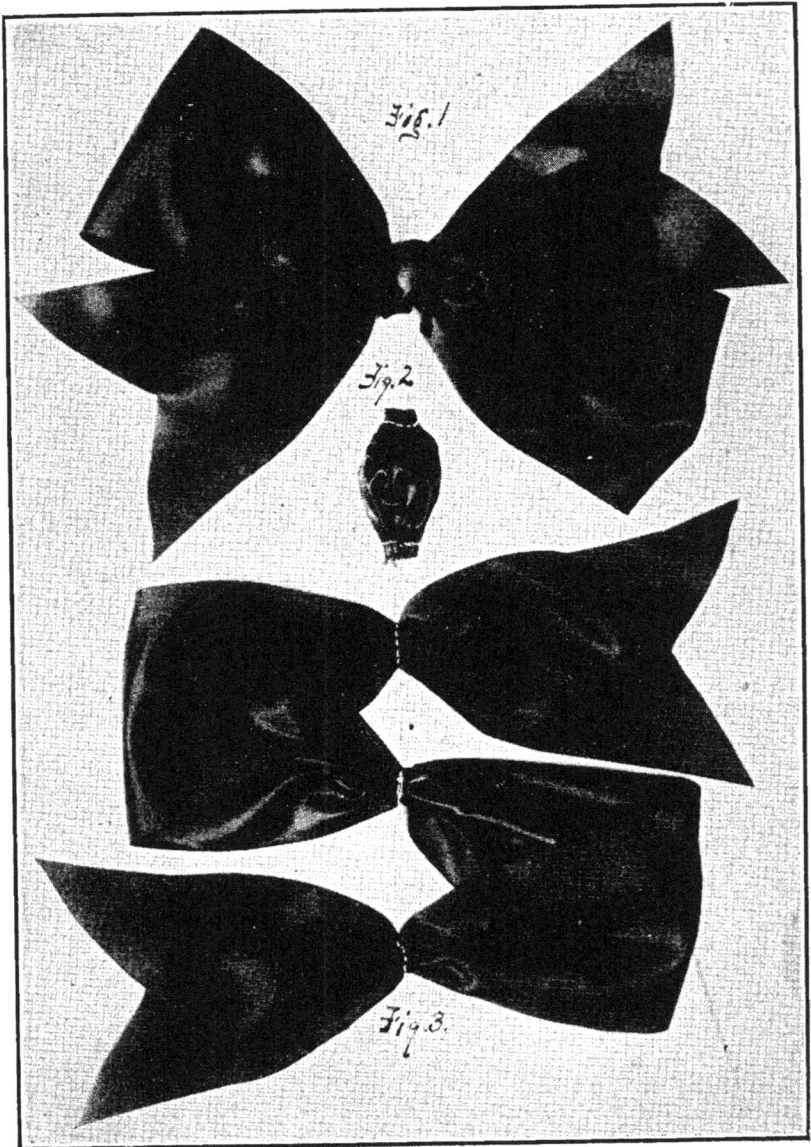

The Alsatian Bow From Start to Finish

one-half inches long, directly behind it. The loop and the end is laid pull it into place with the right thumb on the upper side of the ribbon, and the forefinger on the under side, with only one thickness of silk between them. Then give a gentle but firm stroke parallel to the selvage and away from the plait, and the ribbon will fall into beautiful folds, displaying the lights and shadows of the silk to perfection. Continue these plaits, all folded in the same direction, until the selvage is reached. Sew down the plaits with millinery thread so that they will retain their exact place, and if the plaiting takes too wide a space throw the thread around it and cinch it up, keeping the sewing flat the while, never let it cinch up into a roll.

Next plait the marked place in the center of the ribbon. Here the plaits must be reversed. For if they were made in the same dirction as the first line of plaiting and the two were brought together to make a loop of the ribbon, one side of the selvage would stand wide open and the other would be entirely closed. But if the plaiting is reversed at the second marking the loop will be open equally on both selvages. To make the second plaiting, it is easier for most persons to turn the ribbon around and repeat the process of plaiting exactly the same as it was in the first place. A few persons can go straight down a piece of ribbon plaiting to the right or left indiscriminately. The same side of the ribbon must always be kept uppermost. It is the *effect* we want, and do not care for the method. The third plaiting is reversed from the second.

When it comes to putting the bow together, fold it exactly as you did when laying off the places for plaits. The plaits will all come together in one place, with a loop and an end on either side. Sew the plaits together, one on top of another, and arrange the bow so that the ends will be diagon-

ally across from each other, and the loops the same.   If the
are fastened. at the center of the single Alsatian, so they will
stand straight up from the bow.   The end is sloped from its

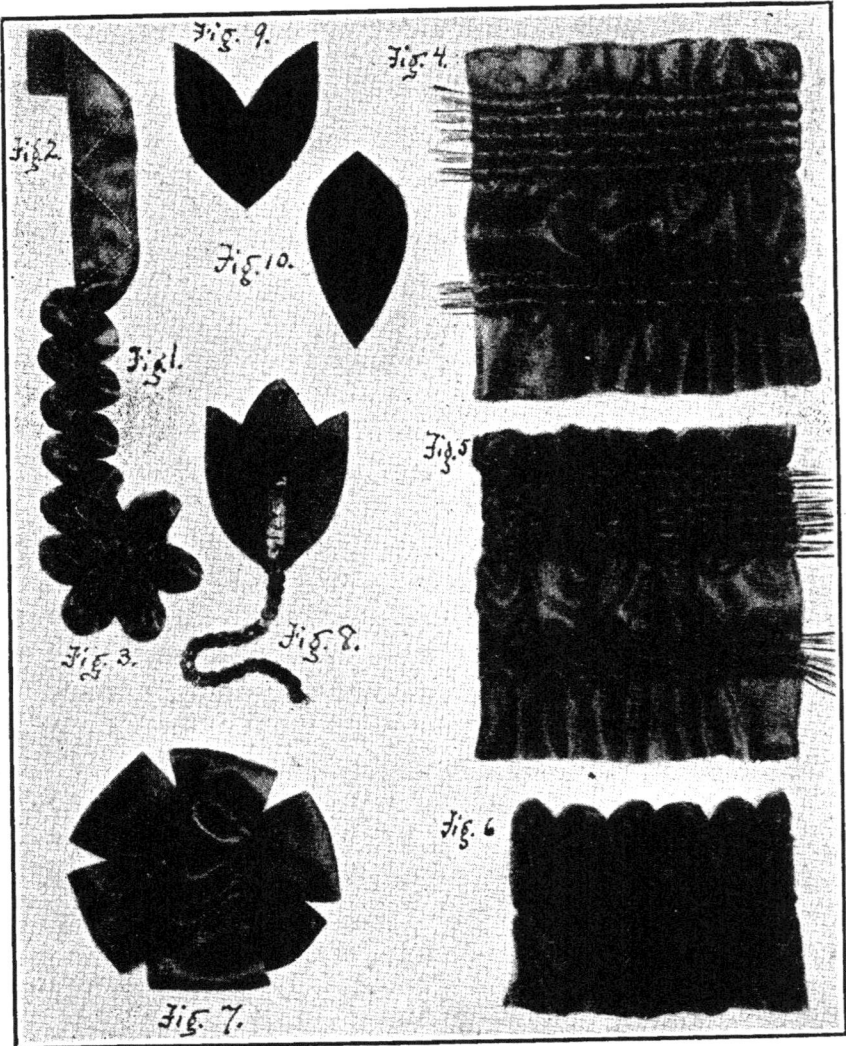

A variety of Fancy Trimmings.   See Text

tip, at one selvage, to the other selvage at the height of the top of the loop. Three centers are used in the same manner as described in making the center of the triple bow, one about the standing part, and one about each plaiting of the single Alsatian bow. These centers are made like all others, only one end is plaited diagonally across the ribbon, making one edge longer than the other. All these longer edges go to the center, where they are caught together with a single stitch and the needle thrust through to the wrong side and thread secured. This completes the standing Alsatian, and it is very useful for trimming the front of a large hat. .

The Maltese Bow

Make two single Alsatian bows of ribbon from two to three inches wide. Lay the bows across each other, at right angles, and fasten them in the center. This makes a Maltese cross in itself. Put the usual plaited piece across the center diagonally, and another like it, at right angles to the first, making another Maltese cross of the centerpieces. This completes a very pretty bow. Maltese bows are usually used in pairs to trim a hat. . One on the left front, and the other at the right back. They should rest against the side crown, with the ends slighly touching the brim. If one of the ribbons comprising the center is parallel with the side crown, the position of the bow is correct. These bows may be of ribbon or ribbon velvet, and a hat would need no other trimming when it has a pair of Maltese bows.

The Shell Edge

The shell edge, shown in Fig. 1, is made of No. 5 ribbon, and gathered with thread to match the ribbon in color. Never use silk or mercerized thread for gathering as they both fray and slip. Use hard twisted cotton No. 50.

Get the diagonal across the ribbon by folding the selvage across its width, as shown in Figure 2. Secure the end of the thread firmly and use a running stitch (see lesson on stitches) which must be small and even. When you get across the diagonal, point the needle so it will go *under* the selvage, and when beginning the next diagonal, commence *above* the selvage, in order that the thread will go around the selvage each time. Otherwise the selvage would flare out, and destroy the unity of the shells. Continue the sewing back and forth diagonally, draw up the thread gently, arrange the shells by forcing the point of a finger under each of them; then see that they are regularly distanced, and not too close together.

Take six shells, all on one side, catch the selvage exactly in the middle of the shells, and from underneath, and draw them together, and fasten them, making the center of the flat rosette shown in Figure 3. The six shells on the outer edge should be evenly disposed, and where they overlap, they are fastened. The rosette may be made independently of the edge, or it may be but a continuation of it.

This shell edge is one of the most useful ornamentations found in millinery. It is pretty around a crown base, over a crown top, about a brim edge, either on the upper or lower side, and makes a fine heading for folds of chiffon, crêpe, or maline. It is useful for ornamenting baby caps, and is one of the most effective trimmings for a dinner waist, around a full-dress neck, or on sleeves, where it terminates in the flat rosette. It finishes the front seams of an evening skirt, and the flat rosette makes an artistic end near the hem. The uses of this simple device are legion, and all are pleasing and beautiful.

The Shell Shirring

The shell shirring shown in Figure 6 is made of thin piece silk. The top is folded over to the width desired for the

130

shells, and a thread run along this line to mark it. It is managed exactly as the ribbon in the shell edge. Diagonal markings are laid off between the upper edge and the marking thread, and these are followed in cotton thread, with the running stitch. Go over the upper edge in the same manner, as the selvage was crossed in the shell edge.

The second line of shirring is made by basting a tuck of the same width as the first row of the shirring. The tuck is then laid off diagonally, and sewed exactly as the first row of shirring. When the threads are drawn up, and the shells pulled into place, by inserting the finger under each one, and the whole is basted to a firm foundation it gives one of the most lovely effects that can be imagined.

The shell shirring is of especial use, in covering a hat brim, on either or both sides, or it can be laid on a side crown, or across the crown top. It is also beautiful on an evening waist, on vest and sleeves.

The Flat Reed Shirring

The flat reed shirring is made of a straight piece of silk, folded back on itself to the width of the shirring desired. In the sample, Figure 4, there are two groups of shirring, so the silk must be folded back far enough to cover both. Leave a margin of the silk at the top, the width of the little ruffle that is wanted for a heading, and run a gathering thread through both thicknesses of the silk to define this width. Do not draw up this thread, but run another under it, and one-quarter of an inch distant from the first. Continue this process until the desired numbers are made. These threads should be securely fastened where they begin, and should all begin from one side. Take a cord, cotton soutache, or common wrapping string, so it is large enough, and run it through a darning needle. Tie a knot in the end, and turn the needle, eye first, and put the cord through the casings made by the stitching in the silk. Keep the silk smooth all the time, never allow it to pucker. Cut off the cord, leaving an inch projection beyond the silk. Run all the casings in this manner. Leave a space of the silk, and run the second group of shirring. This is done exactly like the first only there are but two or three casings in the last group. Put in the cord, and then stitch down all the knots in the cord, so it will not pull through the casings. Pull up the cords, arranging the fulness evenly. Next pull the threads carefully, one by one.

The picture shows a small portion near the thread ends, where the silk is not drawn up, so that the construction may be fully understood.

The Round Reed Shirring

The round reed shirring is made by folding over the silk at the top, sufficiently to run a thread, and make the desired ruffle at the top. After that, the silk is used in a single thickness, and made into tucks. Use three-eighths of an inch of the silk, for each tuck, and space them one-quarter of an inch apart. Make five or any number wanted, leave a space of the silk, and run two or three more tucks. These tucks are run with cord, exactly as in the flat reed shirring, then they are fastened, pulled up, and arranged in the same way. The round reed shirring is shown in Figure 5.

These two shirrings are called *reed* shirrings because in the past they were run with reeds, instead of cords. These reeds were something like rattan.

Reed shirrings will do nicely for hat brims or underfacings, or can be used on evening dresses or waists.

There is a rule for shirrings which is tabulated as follows: Measure the length to be covered with the shirring, and, of velvet it takes one and one-quarter times that length; of silk it takes one and one-half times that length; of chiffon it takes twice that length; of maline it takes' three times that length.

In the case of making these reed shirrings a very thin quality of silk was used, and it took of the silk, one and three-quarter times the distance to be covered.

The Dimpled Rosette

This rosette takes one yard of two-inch ribbon. Cut off twenty inches, space it off into five parts of four inches each, and leave it in one continuous piece. Begin at one end, and plait it, reverse the plaiting at four inches distant, and keep on reversing the plaiting every four inches until the twenty inches are consumed. Turn the ribbon on the wrong side, take the second plaiting, and bring it up to the first, and fasten them together, making a loop. Then comes the third plaiting, which is fastened to the second, and so on to the end of the twenty inches. This gives five loops of four inches each. Take the center loop and bend the top inward, at each selvage, until the selvages meet. Secure them togther with a tie stitch.

Tie-stitch each side of the loop, just where the selvage comes up from the bottom of the loop, and begins to turn in toward the center. Treat the center loop, and the ones on each side of it, in the same way.

This is putting in the dimples.

The remaining sixteen inches of ribbon cut in two pieces. Lay each of these pieces off into two loops of four inches each. Form the loops in the same manner, as the longer piece, and spread them apart, like the ribs of a fan and fasten them on either side of the central loops, so as to make a complete circle of the six flat loops, as shown in Figure 7.

Conventional Lily Bud

The conventional lily bud is used when net and jet need a color motive, which in this case would be the silk under the net. For instance, the bud might be a rich red or orange, and veiled with the black net, and ornamented with the jet circles and stem, it would make a distinguished and striking note on a black hat. The lily is shown in Figure 8 and its pattern is given in Figures 9 and 10.

Endless are the combinations of colors, and the variety of ornaments that can be employed to produce chic and novel effects in millinery.

Checker board Weaving
in Ribbon—a perennial favorite

LESSON XXIII

Shirrings, Rosette and Buckles

(See page 138)

Buckles can be made in any shape—round, square, oblong, oval, or any fancy form. Cut out a pattern the exact size and shape desired, pin it on buckram, and cut the buckram to the pattern. Wire the outer and inner edges of the buckram with lace wire, placing the wire even with the edges, on the rough side of the buckram. If the buckle is to be made of velvet, baste the smooth side of the buckram to the wrong side of the velvet, so that the velvet will project one-quarter of an inch beyond the buckram, around the inner and outer edges. If the form of the buckle will permit, the velvet should be on the bias.

Take the fancy shape shown in Figure 1. First turn down the velvet over one of the blunt outer points, then fold it in from each side of the point, and stitch the velvet through these three turnovers or flaps. The velvet projecting on the inner edge must be slit at the corners and turned up on to the buckram. Do not cut the corners too far up, or they will leave a raw edge through which the buckram foundation will most likely show. Now stitch back and forth as shown in the illustration, and when the bias velvet must be caught from the inner edge be sure and let the needle catch far enough from the raveled edges so that the thread cannot by any chance pull out. Each projecting corner is treated like the first, and the long sides of the buckle are laced together as shown in Figure 1, along with the buckram, wiring and projecting velvet.

Figure 2 shows the completed buckle, ornamented with

soutache braid and jet. A wire can be sewed on the under side, across the opening of the buckle, either lengthwise or cross-wise, and ribbon may be placed over the wire projecting on either side of the buckle.

A buckle can be used to advantage in various places in hat trimming or on belts, coats and dresses. Buckles can be made of straw, silk, satin, velvet, chiffon folds, lace or small flowers, and their beauty enhanced by the addition of beads or embroidery. There is no end to their diversity.

The Plastron Rosette

While this rosette is made of any size, the ribbon should never be over two inches wide, or the center will not make up nicely. First, a round disk is cut from buckram and a dot made in its center. From this dot are drawn radiating lines terminating at the edge. These are used as guides in making the center. Bind the disk with a narrow strip of the ribbon from which the rosette is to be made.

Take one end of the ribbon and plait it in the same manner used in making the loops for bows. Sew this plaited end on the under side of the disk even with the ribbon binding. The under side of the disk is the rough side of the buckram. Bring the ribbon over on the right side of the buckram and leave two inches to form a loop and plait it across the width of the ribbon, reversing from the plaiting at the beginning.

Fasten this plaiting down on the right side of the disk as near to its edge as possible; at the distance of 1 inch from this second plaiting make the third, reversing from the second. When it is completed, push it up nearly to the second, and sew it to the buckram. That process gives the puffs seen in the center. Continue in this manner, reversing the plaiting each time and sewing the puffs down the line toward the center as they are made.

The moment the puffs begin to diverge from the line because of being crowded, cut off the ribbon and begin another row at the edge of the disk, making the loop first and the puffs afterward.

Sometimes only one or two puffs can be made before they diverge from the line, and in any case the row is never carried beyond the center.

Watch that the ribbon is not plaited too closely in making the loop, or it will take up so little space on the edge of the disk that the loops will overlay each other. When clear around the edge the last puff is made by plaiting the end of the ribbon and turning it under and catching it down to the buckram so that it makes a puff like all the rest.

The Plastron Rosette is made large enough to cover the whole top of the crown, or so small it merely holds a quill in place. It is sometimes sewed on the under brim of a large hat at the left back, or it can be used on the girdle. It is one of the most satisfactory rosettes, as it displays the lights and shadows of silk so very effecively. The Plastron Rosette and its construction is shown in Figure 3.

Pin Shirring

The shirring shown in Figure 4 is called pin shirring and is the finest shirring made. It is used in all mourning goods, especially crêpe. It is also a delightful embellishment for a baby bonnet, or the underfacing for a hat. It can be turned to various uses in dressmaking as well.

Pin shirring is composed of a series of small tucks varied according to taste. There may be five or seven tucks, then an interval of plain goods, and another group of two or three tucks.

If the silk is intended for the underfacing of a hat, measure off one inch at the top facing, turn half of it back. That

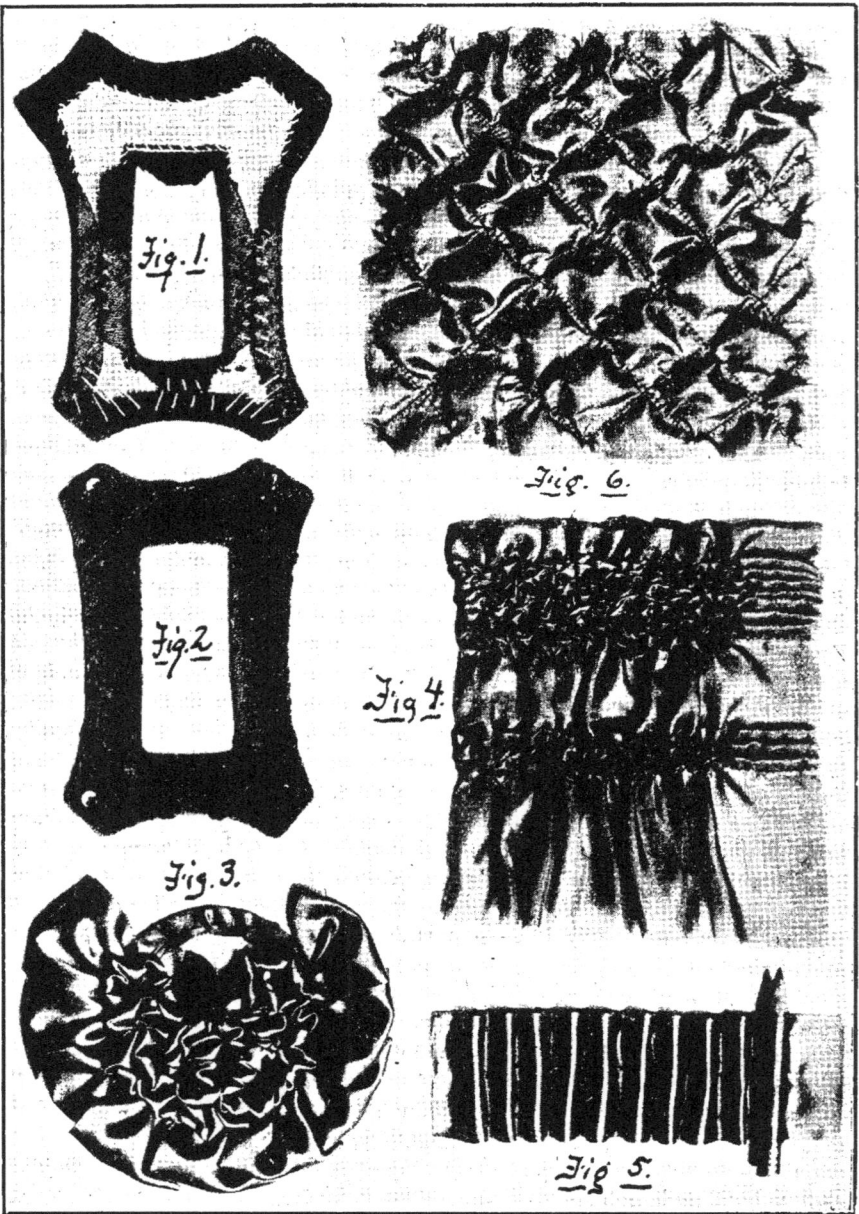

Fig. 1.

Fig. 2

Fig. 3.

Fig. 6.

Fig 4.

Fig. 5.

will make a fold half-inch wide. Run a gathering thread through it, just so far above the raw edge, as will prevent its raveling. This will make a ruffled edge, approximately one-third of an inch wide. The tucks are usually about one-eighth of an inch wide, that is, taking a quarter of an inch of silk, which is doubled when the tuck is formed. Whatever the width of the tucks, it is duplicated in their distance apart. If the tucks are one-eighth of an inch wide, they are placed one-eighth of an inch from each other. They are each run with a drawing thread, which is firmly secured at its beginning, and all tucks are run in the same direction from right to left. There are no cords or strings used in these tucks, but they are simply drawn up by the gathering threads which make the tucks, and the goods will fall into graceful, wavy effects. A small space has been left, without drawing up the threads, so that the constructive stitching may be seen.

With a needle or pin, the fluted and wavy fulness of this shirring, can be equally spaced and made both even and most beautiful.

The quantity of silk required to cover a given space can be ascertained by referring to the table for shirrings.

Cartridge Shirring

This shirring is done over a round pencil, as shown in Figure 5. Only three stitches are required to hold each fluting in place. The ribbon or velvet must be sewed on some stiff background. If it should be buckram, first secure the end of the ribbon to it with three stitches—one in the middle and the other two near the selvage of the ribbon on either side. Place the pencil under the ribbon and bring the needle through the buckram and ribbon, with the needle at exact right angle to the buckram and barely touching the pencil, as it goes upward. If the needle should be in a sloping position it would bring the flutings too close together or too far apart, according to the way the needle was inclined. Make the stitching up one row and down the other until the required length of shirring is made.

The cartridge shirring, if placed around a small crown, makes it *look* large. It can be made upon a bridle, which is merely a piece of buckram laid around the crown and about a half inch away from it. The buckram should be cut the height of the crown and the ends stitched together making a circle. Cover the rough or inner side of the buckram with silk, bringing it over the edge on the side where the shirring is placed. This conceals the buckram entirely. It is preferable to have ribbon velvet for the shirring, as it stays in place better than the plain ribbon and hides the stitching.

The cartridge shirring may be sewed directly on the crown in the manner described if the sides are perpendicular. If the sides are sloping but the line is straight, instead of curved, the shirring can still be used by quilling it around the top first and gradually spreading out each fluting toward the headsize. Keep each fluting in a straight line from the headsize to the crown top.

The cartridge shirring can be introduced in short lengths in a continuous straight hat band, or it can be utilized in dress trimming.

The Honeycomb Shirring

The honeycomb shirring shown in Figure 6 is used primarily for evening hats. Suppose it is to be put on the top of a crown. Cut out the silk, satin or velvet in the shape required, allowing one-quarter extra in length and width for shirring, according to the table given before. Crease a diagonal line across the goods, and others parallel to the first, and about one and one-half inches apart, until it is all laid off in one direction. Now crease a line directly across, and at right angles to the others and make the rest of the lines parallel to this one and one and one-half inches from each other. This lays off the goods into squares.

Take a fine needle and fine thread and with small stitches run the creases that all run one way. Commence with the needle on the same side each time, and see that the thread is firmly secured at the beginning.

After all the threads are run one way turn the goods at right angles, and run the creases from that side, making squares of the fabric. In running the second group of threads be sure and go under the first set, where they cross each other, so that when it comes to drawing up the threads they will run freely from both directions.

Next put the goods on the crown top. Pin the goods at the knots of thread on one side, where the shirring begins, leaving a fulness between the pins, according to the amount given in the shirring table. Draw the threads up, making the fulness one-quarter more than the distance covered, and fasten the ends of the thread about the pin which holds down the goods diagonally across from the place of beginning. After all the threads are secured in one direction, treat the crossing threads in exactly the same manner. With a long pin and a little patience the puffs can be arranged so they will fall into place and can then be easily stitched to stay.

A very ornamental effect is produced by using gold or silver thread for the shirring and sewing a pearl bead wherever the threads cross. A hat with this shirring needs very little trimming, as the needlework is too handsome to hide.

LESSON XXIV

Wiring Ribbon

All bows which have loops that stand upright must be wired. This is done in three different ways. A lace wire can be laid near the edge of the ribbon, and the selvage brought over it, and blind-stitched down with small stitches. This method is shown in Figure 1. Catch the selvage on the very edge, lay it over the wire and take up a thread of the ribbon, just opposite the stitch in the selvage, and draw them together. Then put the point of the needle inside of the fold and take up a thread of the ribbon, simply to draw the sewing thread out of sight, and then repeat the first stitch. If the sewing thread was not drawn back under the flap of the selvage, it would show all the way down the hem. The wire is only used on one side of the ribbon, and should be put in before the loop is made.

In the case of wiring an end, the wire should be extended along one side to the very tip.

The second way of wiring ribbon is shown in Figure 2 where the regular ribbon wire is used. This consists of two or three small wires enclosed in a tape. This wire is caught to the center of the ribbon and can be secured with a feather stitch, or merely by tie-stitching it occasionally. Either stitching should be done on the inside, and only on the back of the loops, and this wiring cannot be used for the ends at all.

The third way to wire ribbon and the most substantial is to make a frame work, as shown in Figure 3, and place the ribbon over it. Let the selvage of the ribbon be far enough away from the wire so that by no chance the wire will be exposed. Tie stitch the wire to the ribbon, three times at the top,

142

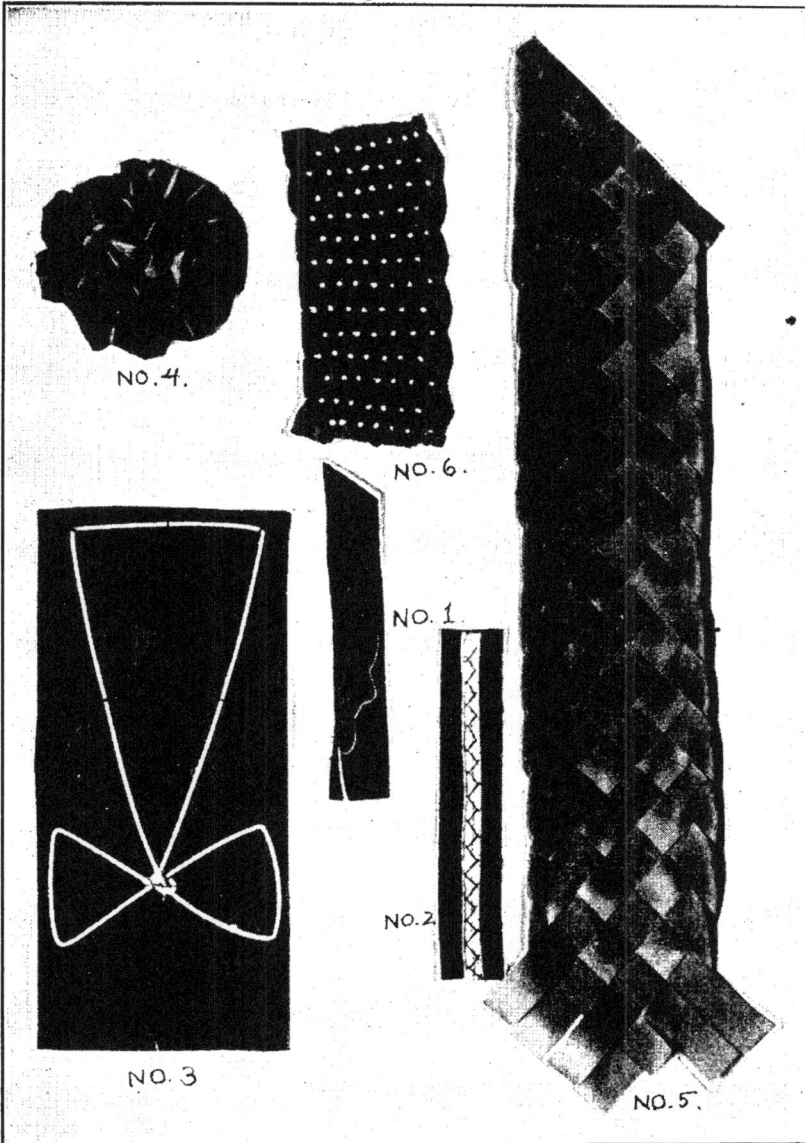

NO.4.

NO.6.

NO.1.

NO.2.

NO.3

NO.5.

Wiring Ribbon and some popular trimmings
Figures 1, 2, 3, 4, 5, 6.   See pages 142 to 147.

143

and at each side, on the back of the loop on the inside. This leaves no stitching on the front of the loop.

In the illustration, the ribbon, which is turned back so as to show the wire framework, should be brought forward over the top wire, plaited and sewed down at the base. Be careful not to draw the ribbon too tightly over the structure, or it looks stiff and loses all expression. Neither must it be too loose, or the front of the loop will flap like a sail.

The two wire flanges shown at the bottom are to be used when the loop of ribbon is upright, on the top of a hat, in which case the flanges are bent around to lie flat on the crown top. The ribbon is eventually draped around the base, so as to conceal the wire structure. It is best to have a piece of buckram sewed underneath the crown top and extending down either side for a firm foundation for the upright loops and wire.

The Simple Rosette

One and three-quarter yards of 4-inch ribbon makes the simple rosette. If the ribbon is wider or narrower, the length of the ribbon required is more or less in proportion. Turn in the ends of the ribbon for one-half inch, and double the whole piece in the center of its length. This throws the two selvages together. Take a millinery needle and stout thread and run it along the length of the ribbon, about one-eighth of an inch from the selvage, going through both thicknesses of the ribbon The stitches should be one-eighth of an inch long. Be sure that the end of the thread is well secured, as all depends upon its strength when the fulness is drawn up. Draw it up as tight as possible and dispose the fulness in four layers, on the under side, where the selvage and gathering come. Formerly a rosette was made by coiling the gathering round and round, but the lights and shadows of the silk are much better displayed by arranging the gathers thus:

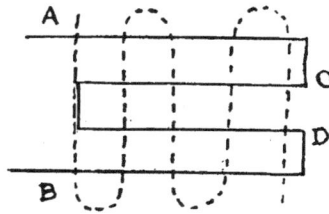

Diagram for making Simple Rosette

Draw up *a* to *b* and stitch them together, also fasten *c* to *d* and the outer lines being longer than the inner ones, a rounded effect is produced which makes the stem of the rosette. After the stem is arranged, run a needle through and through, as shown by the dotted lines. Do not draw it up very tight, but just enough so that no holes will show through the stem when the rosette is turned upright. Do the running stitch where the gathering threads come, not higher, for that closes up the rosette, nor lower, for that will expose the gathering threads. Turn the rosette over, on its stem, and arrange the whole frill by going over it like grandmother used to scallop pie crust edge.

Press the rosette down in the center with a finger point, to see how the frill lies, and there will be found two places where a small tie stitch should be used. One where the ends come together to make the frill continuous, and the other opposite, in the place the doubled stem turns back on itself. The rosette is now finished. When made of light colors in wide ribbon it is very artistic for children's hats, or when in narrow widths for hair decoration, and when very small for waists and dresses. It is shown in Figure 4.

145

A much fuller rosette can be made from the same ribbon by turning in the ends and folding it lengthwise, as described in the first instance, but the gathering thread is run one-eighth of an inch from the middle crease and through the two thicknesses of silk. This throws all the selvages to the edge of the frill. It is not so rich in effect, but fuller.

The Woven Band

The woven band shown in Fig. 5 is made of No. 3 ribbon. It can be made of any width of ribbon or any number of strips can be used. The one in the illustration has seven strips. The ends of the strips are first sewed to a narrow piece of buckram, so closely that they touch each other. The strips are laid out straight, and the one on the left hand is turned up and over at right angles. The second strip is laid over the first, the third is laid under the first, the fourth is put over he first, and so on alternating until the end piece of the first strip lies straight out on the table at right angles to the rest.

The second, and all of the other five strips, are treated exactly as the first. When they all extend at right angles to the rows that were laid out first, take the upper ribbon on the right, bend it up and over on itself at right angles, bring the second over the first, the third under the first, and proceed with them all, as was done in the first instance, working the ribbons back to the left hand side. So the work goes on until the band is made of the required length. An estimate can be made of the *width* by the number of strips used, and of the *length,* by folding one ribbon back and forth on the bias, keeping the folds at right angles, and at the width determined upon, until the length desired is attained. That will give the length of one strip, and it is then easy to estimate how many will be required for the number of strips wanted.

This band is most effectively made of two contrasting colors, pink and blue, gold and red, or of different shades of one color, as purple shading to lavender.

When a sailor hat is trimmed with such a band made of silk or velvet ribbon, closed with a quill and cabochon, it is very fetching.

Smocking

Smocking produces the effect shown in Figure 6. Take the silk or any goods desired, crease it in folds one-quarter of an inch apart. Put the first crease against the second crease, and just even with it. Let the needle pierce from underneath through one crease, and then stitch the second to it, sewing through them both three times, making a small knot. Now run the needle along the first crease underneath for about three-quarters of an inch and pierce it through to the right side, at the top of the crease, and stitch the second crease to it, with three overcast stitches.

Continue in this manner until the first and second creases are fastened together at equal distances. At the end where this is finished thrust the needle through the second crease, half way between the knots of thread already made. Draw up the third crease to the second and overcast with three stitches. Slip along the under side of the second crease, again equally distant between the knots of thread in the first and second creases. Pierce through the second crease at its top and bring up the third crease and stitch the second and third together. Continue in this manner to the end of the second and third creases. The third and fourth creases are sewed together exactly opposite the first and second, and the fourth and fifth are fastened opposite the second and third, and this process is repeated until the required amount of smocking is made. It is beautiful for the tops of crowns, especially on evening toques. In the latter case it may be stitched with gold thread or heavy embroidery silk in the same or contrasting colors of the silk or satin upon which it is used. Small beads are sometimes introduced where the joining of the creases is made.

Hat bands often have an inset of smocking, and for neck yokes of waists or bands on the sleeves nothing is prettier.

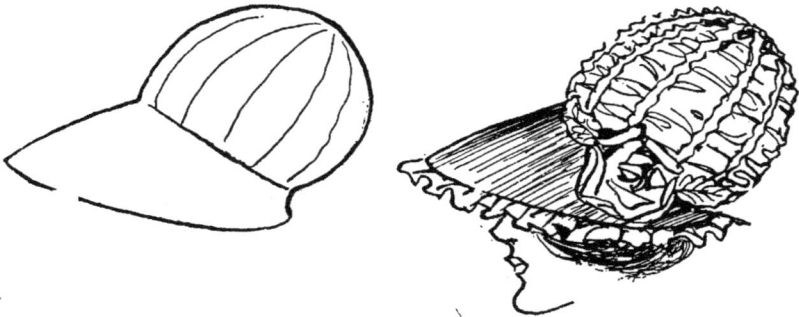

A modernized version of the First Empire Hat, characterized by hand work— Shirring, Plaiting and Smocking.

LESSON XXV

Bows and Rosettes

Figure 1 is the Triple Bow, because everything about it is in groups of three.

There are three groups of loops, with three loops in each group, and three centers, as a finishing touch to this bow. It takes one and three-quarter yards of ribbon three inches wide to make the triple bow. The short loop is made of five and one-half inches, and the two loops under it, take respectively six inches and six and one-half inches. The two under loops can

No. 1 The Triple Bow. Formed by three clusters of three loops.

be made in one continuous piece, the loops separated out, and stitched so they will stay that way, when the short loop is placed over them.

When the three groups are made, fasten them together at their base, merely stitching the edges together, leaving a hole in the center. Otherwise it cramps the center. Each loop must be made with little plaits at its base, all laid in the same direction and pulled into place, by putting the thumbs on the upper side of the ribbon, and the forefinger on the under side, with only one thickness of the silk between the thumbs and finger, and then give a gentle but firm stroke parallel to the selvage of the ribbon, and away from the plaits, and the ribbon will fall into beautiful folds, displaying the light and shadow of the silk to perfection.

The other end of the loop must be plaited in the same manner, only the plait must lie in the opposite direction.

When these two ends are brought together to form the loop it will be found that the selvage of both sides will part equally. Whereas, if both ends were plaited alike, one side of the selvage would stand wide open, and the other would be tightly closed.

The center is composed of three separate strips, which go individually around each group. The end of one of these center pieces is plaited very fine, so as to take little space, and straight across the width of the ribbon. The other end is plaited in the same way, but slightly diagonal, so as to make the upper selvage shorter than the lower. Each time that a plait is made on the diagonal, it is reversed in direction from the first plaiting, and as you hold it firmly in the right hand, run your middle finger from underneath to the middle of the center, allowing only one thickness of the silk over the finger. This produces the fluted effect, in the middle of each center. The lower edge of the center, being longer than the upper edge, it extends downward, so that a needle may be drawn through the exact middle of the bow, and the three selvages, from the three drooping edges of the centers, can be caught with one stitch each, drawn together, and sewed fast on the wrong side. One hole will be visible in the middle of the bow.

This bow is useful for the hat, and may be turned into a stickup, by doubling the length of the loops in one group.

The triple bow looks well on the corsage and can be used in many delightful ways.

Double Butterfly

The Double Butterfly Bow, shown in Figure 2, takes one and one-half yards of three-inch ribbon for its construction.

No. 2. The double Butterfly Bow; an effective trimming simply constructed.

The two standing pieces are cut separately. The lower one is sixteen inches long. Double it in the middle, across its

151

width and measure off four inches from this center, along one of the selvages. Turn down the ends diagonally to the eight-inch selvage point and cut off the ends along this slope. If the line along which you cut is slightly curved outward, it will add to the artistic effect, although it be scarcely discernible to the eye.

Next plait the piece along the middle line, in very fine plaits and throw the thread around them, and cinch them up. Turn up the pointed ends so they face each other, and throw one more loop of the thread around the center, just above the plaiting to make a little stem.

The second standing piece is made exactly like the first, but its length is fourteen and one-half inches. This doubled in the middle, gives two pieces seven and one-quarter inches long. Mark off three and one-eighth inches, from the center, along one selvage, and cut to the point of the seven and one-quarter inch selvage. From this the process is identical with the first standing piece.

The second piece is now laid over the first one, and stitched down. A small tie stitch in each piece secures the ends and makes the proper parting of the points at the top.

A piece of ribbon twenty-two inches long, is divided into five parts, each one being four and one-half inches in length. This is kept in one continuous piece. It is plaited and stroked as before described, at one end of the ribbon, and the plaiting reversed at the first four and one-half inches, and this alternating is repeated every four and one-half inches until the whole piece is used. Turn it on the wrong side, bring the second plaiting up to the first end and stitch them together, making a loop. Form the next loop, and stitch it at its base to the second plaiting, the fourth to the third and so on to the end.

This gives five loops, more or less elastic, so they can be arranged in a half moon about the base of the standing pieces, or they may be alternated, one inclining upward and the next downward, or they may be in a straight row. In any event, catch the middle loop first in its position, at the center of the base of the uprights, and then curve the ends, as desired, and stitch in place. If the loops were sewed solidly together, they would not give, but would stay in a solid lump.

The double butterfly, if used as a stickup, must be wired along the inner selvage of the standing pieces. This can be done before they are plaited, simply bringing the selvage over the wire on to the wrong side, and blind-stitching it down.

The Aeroplane Bow

The Aeroplane Bow, shown in Figure 3, requires fourteen inches of ribbon two and one-half inches wide. It is made

No. 3 The Aeroplane Bow

in two pieces. The lower one is the longer. It is seven and one-half inches in length. Double it in the middle, measure off 2 inches from the center along one selvage, and slope the ends, as in the Double Butterfly. The smaller piece is 5 inches in length, double it, across its width, mark off one and one-eighth inches along one selvage, from the double, and slope its ends in like manner to the first.

These two pieces are plaited very small, in their centers, and laid side by side with the short edges together.

Fasten them by a few stitches on the edge of the center of each piece, and take a separate piece of ribbon to cover this stitching, and complete the bow. This should be plaited at the top so that it would spread out ,and then the plaiting should be reversed at the bottom, and drawn very tightly together so as to give this center of the bow a heart-like appearance.

Four of these bows, about the crown of a hat, and connected by a ribbon whose plaited ends are hidden under the bows, make a snappy trimming. The bows are placed equally distant from each other starting at the left front, and are so disposed on the side crown that the longer ends lie partly on the brim.

The Sunflower Rosette

The Sunflower Rosette, shown in Figure 4, takes three yards of ribbon, anywhere from one and one-half to two inches wide. If you ask for ribbon one and one-half inches wide, you will be told there is no ribbon made of that width, and if you ask for two-inch ribbon, it will not measure that the rosette. Cut sixteen pieces, each six inches long. This requires two and two-thirds yards of the ribbon. Each of these pieces must be fishtailed at either end. This is done by folding the ribbon in the middle, lengthwise, so the two selvages come together, then at the end, bend the center of the ribbon out to the selvage, so that the upper edge of the end will lie parallel and just over the selvage. Cut across the diagonal double, and it gives the notched effect called fishtailing. Next fold the ribbon in the middle, from top to bottom, and then fold again across its center, from side to side. Bend the notched ends upward together and then part them out, until one overlaps the other, for about one-third of its width. This is shown in the first fold of ribbon, at the side of the rosette. Take one small plait at the bottom, as shown in the second

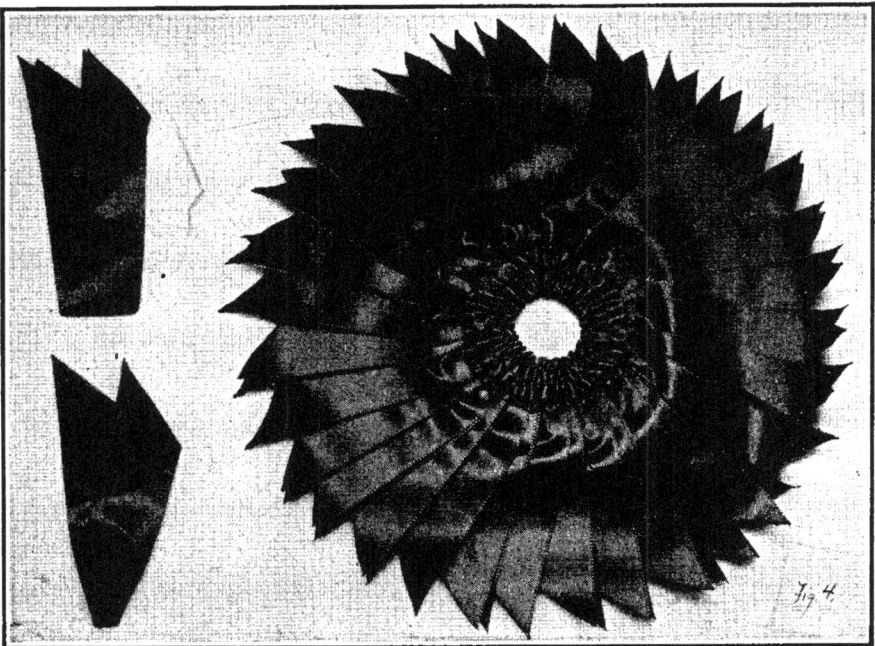

No. 4. Sunflower rosette.

fold of ribbon, and stitch it in place. All sixteen pieces are similarly treated, observing carefully all the while, that all the points of the rosette are in the same direction that the overlapping end always comes from the same side, and that the plait at the bottom is of the same depth, and in the same direction, with each part.

155

The sixteen pieces are then laid together, overlapping each other at the bottom, by half their width. When the lower part is sewed into a ring, the upper part is tie stitched into position, about half way from the center to the outer or notched edge. The tie stitch is made through the lower side of each notched piece, and merely pierces one thickness below it, so no stitches are visible from the outside.

,This rosette is supposed to be made of yellow satin ribbon, and the center covered with a brown velvet button, made over a wooden mold, however, it can be made of ribbon of any color, and finished in the center with a piece of the ribbon shirred in the middle, and once on each side, and drawn up to fit around the central hole, as shown in the diagram.

Two of these rosettes, made in contrasting colors, may be used on a crown top to good effect, half of each one resting flat on the crown top, and the other half sticking straight up like a cock's comb. The rosette is appropriate for a wide brim, or made of smaller ribbon, it can cover a quill end.

The Tailored Ladder Bow

The Tailored Ladder Bow, shown in Figure 5, is made of ribbon the same width as that of the sunflower rosette. Each bow requires five and one-quarter inches of ribbon. Turn in one-quarter of an inch at each end, as shown in the piece of constructive ribbon "A," turn under the lower corner, and bring down this end, along the lower selvage, as also shown in "A." Now double the bow lengthwise, and the flap that comes over to the lower selvage must be fastened by inserting the needle from the back about the center of the side of the flap, and let the needle pass along in the diagonal fold of the side of the flap, until it is very near the bottom, where it should pierce the ribbon on to the wrong side, where it can be secured. Both ends of the bow, being finished in this way, the center is put on perfectly flat, and should be of the same width of the bow. These bows may be used in groups of three and connected by a ribbon, folded to the exact width of the bow center.

A totally different effect can be given by making two little plaits under the bow center, both laid in the same direc-

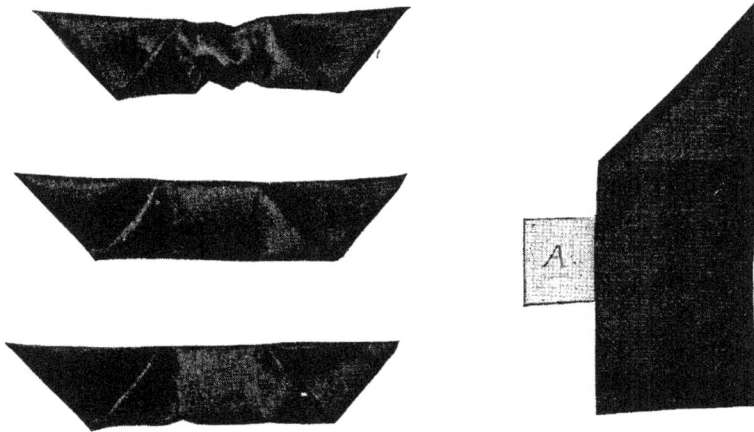

No. 5 The Tailored Ladder Bow

tion. The center, also, has one plait at each end reversed from each other, which raises the middle slightly.

These bows may be used singly, in pairs, or threes; the connecting piece may be omitted and they can be made of silk, velvet, leather, or any fabric, that is not transparent. They are unique for the corsage of a dress, or singly, can be worn at the neck.

The Water Lily Rosette

The Water Lily Rosette is made of one and one-half or two-inch ribbon. There are sixteen pieces, each five and one-half inches long, which are fish-tailed, as in the sunflower rosette. Take each of these pieces, and lay them in two plaits, lengthwise, each plait taking half the width of the ribbon. Let the plaits be in the same direction, and press them in place with a moderate iron. Take two pieces, lay them across each other, at right angles, and stitch firmly together, in the center. Two more pieces, at right angles are placed over the first ones, so as to space this beginning of the rosette into eight parts. Then the rosette is built up, always with two pieces at right angles, so spaced as to fill all the interstices

No. 6. Water-lily Bow.

A smart hat trimming, always in style

of the ends. The last four pieces are caught with the thread over their center, and cinched down firmly in the middle of the rosette. Too much stress cannot be laid upon the necessity of using very strong thread and pulling it very tight in this construction.

After the rosette is sewed, go over each petal with the fingers, pulling it sharply upward and arranging the general appearance artistically, when it will be found to closely resemble the water lily, from which it gets its name.

This is a very pretty rosette for children's hats, or for the hair. It can be made in different shades of the same color, or in contrasting colors. It is useful to the milliner to use up short ends of ribbon. This rosette is shown in Figure 6.

LESSON XXV

The Fancy Alsatian Bow

The Fancy Alsatian Bow is made of two pieces of three-inch ribbon, each of which is eight and one-half inches long. The ends are all fishtailed, and both pieces plaited, in the middle of their length. They are then laid across each other, so

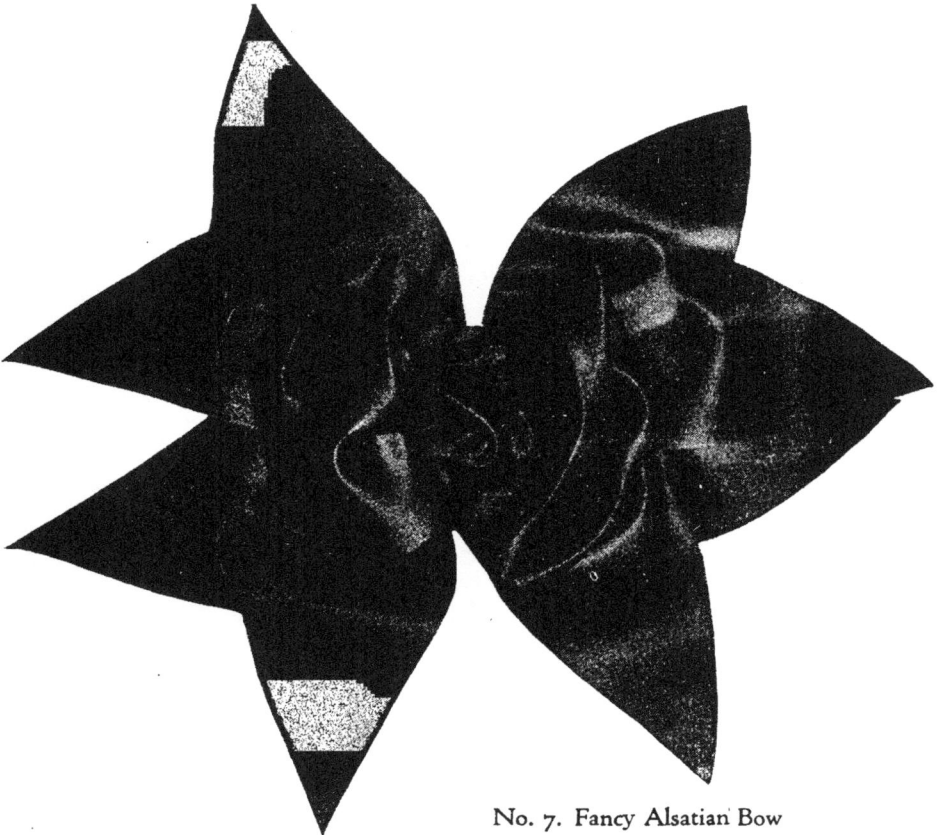

No. 7. Fancy Alsatian Bow

the ends will be slightly apart. Sew the two pieces together, where they cross each other. Take fifteen inches of the ribbon,

159

and lay it off in five sections of three inches each. Plait it exactly as in the Double Butterfly Bow, but do not bend it into a crescent. Place the loops in the center of the two crossed pieces, and sew down the middle loop first, then the end ones. The central loop can be curved like the letter "S," and its ends stitched down, so that it will retain its shape. This bow, when made larger, is beautiful for hat trimming, or made of narrower ribbon or velvet is fine for the neck.

A version of the Alsatian
Bow, used as front trimming

A novelty Butterfly Bow, cleverly
placed

LESSON XXVI

Renovating Stocks

Either the private pupil or the professional milliner will find it invaluable to understand renovation. After a season in which much of the stock has been stored away, the milliner finds material creased, flowers flattened, and feathers out of shape; it is a great satisfaction to know how to restore them to their first freshness.

Put water in a tea kettle, so that it will barely reach the point where the spout begins. Always have the spout perfectly free to conduct the greatest quantity of steam. Suppose it is new velvet which has become badly creased: as soon as the kettle steams with force, let two persons hold the velvet, one at either end, and do not take a space of more than a yard at once. Clasp it on the selvage, in the four places necessary to hold it spread out firm and smooth. Pass it over the steam as near the spout as possible not to touch it. If it is touched by the spout it may make a line on the velvet. Pass the velvet back and forth over the steam, at all times holding it very taut and firm. The back of the velvet should in all cases be next to the spout, and the steam pressing through the fabric raises the nap, and erases all evidences of crease.

When this is accomplished, be very careful not to touch the nap of the velvet, for it is saturated with moisture, and will easily press down. Lay the piece on a table until it dries. If there are other creases, repeat the process till it is all smooth.

Steaming Velvet

If the velvet has been used before, and the creases come from wear, they are harder to eradicate, but it only takes time and patience. If repeated efforts as described do not take out the creases, heat an iron moderately hot, rub a damp cloth over the back of the velvet, and pass the velvet over the face of the iron, as it sets up straight on the table. This will sometimes raise the nap, and obliterate the lines, when nothing else will, as the steam is then generated in the velvet itself. Care must be taken that the material is not bent around the iron too much, or it will make new lines on the iron's edge. Silks and other fabrics can be renovated the same as velvet.

Steaming Velvet Hats

If a velvet hat looks dowdy, it can be steamed on the outside, but not so as to soften the buckram on which it rests. Passing rapidly through the steaming vapor, so it will only touch the outside, and watching that no thumb marks are left, the hat will be greatly improved. Another method is to take a common paint brush, dip it in gasoline, and brush the velvet with it This not only freshens the velvet, but cleans it also. Braids, provided they are not filled with too much sizing, are greatly benefited by slight application of steam.

Treating Maline and Chiffon

So much light filmy material is thrown away that is capable of being turned to good use if the possessor but understood renovation. Take maline and chiffon for example: if they are held firmly and treated exactly like the velvet, they will smooth out and can be used for retrimming. They do not require so much steam as the velvet, for the slight stiffening they possess readily melts before the steam, and only takes a moment to reset.

Very often the edge of the maline has to be cut off because it cannot be held so the steam can straighten it without burning the fingers. That is something that always must be guarded against. Maline has a raw edge anyway, so it does no harm to cut the edge with scissors. Try renovating a chiffon veil and see how greatly it will be improved.

Renovating Flowers

Flowers are fine subjects for renovation. If they are new and only shopworn, a slight breath of steam and a touch of shaping fingers will restore them perfectly. If they are crushed and dirty, a bowl of gasoline will cleanse them. If it is a rose, turn petals downward and souse the flower up and down until clean. If one bath does not do it to satisfaction, try another, and even then, if it still shows streaks, they will disappear in after treatment. *Never* take the flower from the gasoline to the steam, or you will have a fire. Clean them one day, and let them air till the next. If the cloth of the flower is of good substance, silk, batiste, linen, velvet or chiffon, it will come out beautifully when finished. Some of the very ravelly, sleazy flowers, no one could better, and if they are stiff and filled with paint it is the same. The flowers that are soiled from use should first be thoroughly cleaned with gasoline and dried. The next day put them to steam and work with them straightening the petals and getting good form for the flower. Mix tube paint, the kind used for landscapes and portraits, with gasoline, until the tint or shade is made that is desired. Dip in the flowers, turning them and looking to see how the dye is taking.

To Mix the Colors

It will be best to mix these colors with a bristle brush and pour off into a bottle and cork very tight. If it is done in a bowl, at the time of coloring, there is apt to be particles of undissolved color at the bottom, and if it adheres to the flower, it makes a dark splotch. If it has to be done quickly, mix the color and gasoline with a bristle brush and strain through a very thin cloth. The work must be done swiftly as the gasoline evaporates very fast. Pour more gasoline in if the solution diminishes too rapidly.

Tinting Flowers

Let us suppose it is a rose of batiste we are coloring: We dip it and make it a delightful pink, first. Then take a little camel's hair brush and mix a bit of the tube paint on the side of the bowl, making a darker shade, and touch the center of the rose, and a streak in the middle of the petals, from the stamens toward the point of the petal, going but half way the length. Do this while the rose is yet very damp, and the color will diffuse and blend perfectly. If the petals of the rose are to be darkened on the edge alone, immerse the flower first in the color for the body of the rose, then have a saucerful mixed of a darker hue, turn the rose with the petals down, and merely dip the tips in the second solution before the first is dry. Place the rose on the edge of a table or shelf, and set an iron on the stem, so that the rose will hang downward till dry. The edges of the petals may need attention after the flower is perfectly dry. Take a small pair of scissors and clip off all projecting threads, but do not go around the petal in a continuous cut and leave it looking like it had been shaved. Take the small clips with the scissors held at different angles, or if the cut has to take all the edge, pass the edge between the forefinger and thumb, afterwards fluting it outward a little, and this will dispose the threads so the petal will not look too set. If the form of the rose has been injured by the coloring process, after it is perfectly dry it can be re-formed by steam. The steam will not injure the color. Should the rose be half blown, and open too much with steam, put a little rubber band around it until it dries. Should the flowers be small and surrounded with foliage, so that it is not easy to dip them in color, apply the paint with a camel's hair brush.

White Flowers Color Best

White flowers necessarily color best, but all light ones even when shaded, take the paints in a very satisfactory manner; and even dark flowers that have some light spaces are greatly improved.

The green leaves of foliage will only stand a touch of steam, when they can be smoothed out with the fingers. If separated from the wire in the middle of the leaf, apply a little adhesive. Feathers can be renovated by passing through a vigorous spout of steam very quickly and then shaking in warm air. Be careful not to wet them too much with the steam.

Cleaning Laces

Black lace can be cleaned with pure gasoline, and when rinsed in a second bowl usually looks better than when purchased, as all evidence of the sizing is washed from the back of the lace, without diminishing its crispness. Fold the lace until it will conveniently go into a bowl and souse it up and down, until thoroughly washed. Black mesh veils can be renovated the same way. Silk in ribbons or yard goods can be beautifully colored with tube paint and gasoline. A white scarf of silk, maline, or chiffon can be given shaded ends, by dipping the end first in gasoline, and then in two shades of the color, which will blend when the ends are damp. White lace can be made to take most attractive colors, and is one of the most satisfactory fabrics to renovate. Clean it with gasoline first, if it is soiled, and immerse it, all at once, in the paint, so that it will color evenly. The color when damp is more vivid than when it is dry so allowance must be made for that fact.

Dyes to Match

A fashionable dressmaker matches laces to the color of her dresses. She buys a fine cotton lace, colors it, uses small beads, and heavy embroidery silk to outline the design and charges dollars per yard in the bill, where it costs her cents; but her knowledge and artistic taste have made an original thing of beauty, well worth the money..*

Some hat braids take these colors nicely, and some not Be very careful that no drop of water gets into the coloring, or it would spoil everything. In the use of these colors, too much stress cannot be laid upon the danger of mixing fire and gasoline. Never on any account bring the gasoline near a blaze and do not try to re-form the flowers that have been colored until they have dried for a day.

To Mix the Colors

The following list gives the names of the tube paints, and the coloring they will produce by mixture with gasoline:

Tube Paint	Color Prduced
Mauve	Violet
Naples Yellow	Cream Color
Geranium Lake	Pink
Prussian Blue	Light Blue
Black	Gray
Burnt Umber	Brown
Lake and White	Rose
White and Brown	Chestnut
White, Blue and Lake	Purple
Purple Lake	Lavender
Indigo and Lamp Black	Lead Color
Black and Venetian	Chocolate
White and Green	Bright Green
Light Green and Black	Dark Green

Red and Yellow .... Orange
White and Yellow ...... Straw Color
White, Blue and Black ...... Pearl Gay
Chinese Blue .... Chinese Cloth Color
Chrome Green .... Nile Green
Raw Sienna .... Yellow Brown
Deep Chrome ....Bright Yellow
Alizarin Carmine .... Bright Red
Venetian Red .... Brick Red

---

* Velvet, chiffon, maline, batiste and cotton laces color the best of any fabrics.

CAUTION.—*Do not use gasoline in a room where there is a lamp or gas burning or a fire. Never strike a match in the same room where the gasoline mixture is being used!*

CPSIA information can be obtained
at www.ICGtesting.com
Printed in the USA
BVHW03s2258030518
515233BV00006B/53/P

9 781332 115150